CHOCOLATE
COOKERY

Mable Hoffman
CHOCOLATE
COOKERY

Hamlyn
London · New York · Sydney · Toronto

This edition published in 1983 by
The Hamlyn Publishing Group Limited
London · New York · Sydney · Toronto
Astronaut House, Feltham, Middlesex, England

ISBN 0 600 32331 5

Cover photograph by Martin Brigdale
Illustrations by The Hayward Art Group

Filmset in 11 on 12pt Monophoto Garamond by
Servis Filmsetting Limited, Manchester
Printed in Denmark

Contents

Useful Facts and Figures

Notes on metrication

In this book quantities are given in metric and Imperial measures. Exact conversion from Imperial to metric measures does not usually give very convenient working quantities and so the metric measures have been rounded off into units of 25 grams. The table below shows the recommended equivalents.

Ounces	Approx g to nearest whole figure	Recommended conversion nearest unit of 25
1	28	25
2	57	50
3	85	75
4	113	100
5	142	150
6	170	175
7	198	200
8	227	225
9	255	250
10	283	275
11	312	300
12	340	350
13	368	375
14	396	400
15	425	425
16 (1 lb)	454	450
17	482	475
18	510	500
19	539	550
20 (1¼ lb)	567	575

Note: When converting quantities over 20 oz first add the appropriate figures in the centre column, then adjust to the nearest unit of 25. As a general guide, 1 kg (1000 g) equals 2.2 lb or about 2 lb 3 oz. This method of conversion gives good results in nearly all cases, although in certain pastry and cake recipes a more accurate conversion is necessary to produce a balanced recipe.

Liquid measures   The millilitre has been used in this book and the following table gives a few examples.

Imperial	Approx ml to nearest whole figure	Recommended ml
¼ pint	142	150 ml
½ pint	283	300 ml
¾ pint	425	450 ml
1 pint	567	600 ml
1½ pints	851	900 ml
1¾ pints	992	1000 ml (1 litre)

Spoon measures   All spoon measures given in this book are level unless otherwise stated.

Can sizes   At present, cans are marked with the exact (usually to the nearest whole number) metric equivalent of the Imperial weight of the contents, so we have followed this practice when giving can sizes.

Oven temperatures

The table below gives recommended equivalents.

	°C	°F	Gas Mark
Very cool	110	225	¼
	120	250	½
Cool	140	275	1
	150	300	2
Moderate	160	325	3
	180	350	4
Moderately hot	190	375	5
	200	400	6
Hot	220	425	7
	230	450	8
Very hot	240	475	9

Notes for American and Australian users

In America the 8-oz measuring cup is used. In Australia metric measures are now used in conjunction with the standard 250-ml measuring cup. The Imperial pint, used in Britain and Australia, is 20 fl oz, while the American pint is 16 fl oz. It is important to remember that the Australian tablespoon differs from both the British and American tablespoons; the table below gives a comparison. The British standard tablespoon, which has been used throughout this book, holds 17.7 ml, the American 14.2 ml, and the Australian 20 ml. A teaspoon holds approximately 5 ml in all three countries.

British	American	Australian
1 teaspoon	1 teaspoon	1 teaspoon
1 tablespoon	1 tablespoon	1 tablespoon
2 tablespoons	3 tablespoons	2 tablespoons
3½ tablespoons	4 tablespoons	3 tablespoons
4 tablespoons	5 tablespoons	3½ tablespoons

An Imperial/American guide to solid and liquid measures.

Imperial	American
Solid measures	
1 lb butter or margarine	2 cups
1 lb flour	4 cups
1 lb granulated or castor sugar	2 cups
1 lb icing sugar	3 cups
8 oz rice	1 cup
Liquid measures	
¼ pint liquid	⅔ cup liquid
½ pint	1¼ cups
¾ pint	2 cups
1 pint	2½ cups
1½ pints	3¾ cups
2 pints	5 cups (2½ pints)

NOTE: When making any of the recipes in this book, only follow one set of measures as they are not interchangeable.

The World's Favourite Flavour

No other flavour has ever rivalled chocolate in universal appeal. Since the days of Montezuma when the Aztecs drank it from golden goblets in elaborate ceremonies, chocolate has been held in high esteem. The cocoa beans that Cortez brought back to Spain were so highly prized they were kept secret from the rest of Europe for nearly a century. Eventually its popularity spread and drinking chocolate, the only form in which it was served, became very fashionable. In the late seventeenth century cafés serving chocolate drinks sprang up in England and Holland, but it wasn't until the nineteenth century that the Swiss developed a method of making solid milk chocolate.

The enchantment of chocolate has grown through the years. Thanks to the ingenuity of today's chocolate manufacturers, the selection of chocolate products is almost overwhelming. This book describes the principal products to make it easier for you to choose which to use for a particular recipe, and we have tried to give you a representative group of recipes using each of these chocolate products. These recipes have been carefully tested with the kind of chocolate indicated in each, so remember, if you try the recipe with another chocolate, you will probably get slightly different results.

How to Melt Chocolate

Melting chocolate is not as simple as putting chocolate in a saucepan and placing it on the stove until you're ready for it. *Never* leave chocolate on the heat unless you are close by. Chocolate scorches easily and, once scorched, cannot be used.

There are four ways to melt chocolate successfully. Choose the one that's best for you and proceed with care.

Use extra care to melt chocolate over direct heat.

To melt chocolate in your oven, be sure the oven is off.

Over hot water Place the chocolate in the top of a double boiler. Place the top of the double boiler over hot but *not* boiling water until the chocolate is almost melted. Remove the top of the double boiler from the hot water and stir the chocolate until smooth. For small amounts, place the chocolate in a custard cup or small bowl, then set the cup or bowl in a pan of hot but not boiling water until chocolate is almost melted. Remove the cup or bowl from the water; stir the chocolate until smooth.

In a microwave oven Place chocolate in a custard cup or glass measuring cup. Heat in the microwave oven for 1 or 2 minutes. The time varies with the amount of chocolate.

Over direct heat This must be handled very carefully. Melt chocolate in a small heavy saucepan over very low heat, stirring constantly. Remove from the heat as soon as the chocolate melts. Or, set the saucepan with chocolate over the pilot light; stir occasionally until melted.

In the oven Place a small ovenproof bowl with the chocolate in the oven after the oven has been turned off and is no longer hot but still warm. Check the chocolate frequently to be sure it's not burning.

Tips for Melting Chocolate

● Unsweetened chocolate has a tendency to liquefy when melted, but sweet cooking and milk chocolate will hold their shapes when melted until stirred.

● Chocolate melts easier and faster when cut into chunks or small pieces.

● *Never* add water to melting chocolate unless specified in the recipe. Water will not make chocolate more liquid. Instead it will cause chocolate to stiffen and prevent it from being smooth. If melted chocolate is too thick, thin it with a small amount of lard.

● Don't try to hurry the melting process by turning up the heat. High temperatures will thicken or scorch the chocolate.

● Chocolate will continue to melt after it is removed from heat, so you can partly melt it, remove it from heat, then stir until smooth.

The Main Types of Chocolate Products

The main ingredients of chocolate are cocoa, cocoa butter and sugar, and the properties and flavour of chocolate depend on the varying proportions of these.

Plain chocolate
A dark, strong-flavoured chocolate which may be bitter or sweetened, and contains about 35 per cent minimum cocoa solids. Plain chocolate can be eaten on its own or used for baking and cake decoration.

Milk chocolate
This is lighter, and has a less strong flavour than plain chocolate, as milk is added to the sweetened chocolate during manufacture, and the final product contains a minimum of 20 per cent milk solids and 20 per cent cocoa solids. It can be eaten as it is or used for cooking.

Chocolate drops
These are available in milk or plain chocolate, and can be easily melted in a basin over hot water because of their small size. They are ideal for cake decoration or desserts and are also useful in cakes and biscuits where 'chips' of chocolate are required as the pieces of chocolate remain whole during cooking.

Chocolate menier
This has a higher cocoa content (47 per cent minimum cocoa solids) than ordinary plain chocolate, which gives it a darker colour and stronger flavour.

Dipping chocolate
Sometimes referred to as 'couverture' in cookery books, this is good quality 'chocolate flavoured coating' and two types are available: light and dark. It has a high fat content (30 per cent minimum) which makes it ideal for coating chocolates as it gives a glossy appearance, and is less sweet than ordinary chocolate.

Cake coverings
These are chocolate flavoured coatings made mainly from sugar, vegetable fat and flavourings and cannot be used as a substitute for chocolate in cooking. However, they are cheap and can be used for covering cakes and for making decorations such as chocolate leaves. They are available in plain and milk chocolate flavour, and varieties such as chocolate-and-orange.

Cocoa
This is a dry, fine powder which has a bitter taste and needs the addition of sugar. It can be used as flour in cakes and choux pastry, and also added to meringues

and buttercream. It can also be made into a drink with sugar and hot milk, and sweetened varieties are available on the market.

Chocolate spreads

These are made mainly from sugar, vegetable oils and flavourings and have a thick but spreadable consistency, and can be used as a spread or in baking; they are particularly useful as a filling for cakes.

Chocolate flavoured sugar strands

Made from sugar and flavourings, these are good for decorating cakes and biscuits, and can be added to cake mixes to give a speckled effect.

Dessert toppings

These have a pouring consistency and can be used as a sauce for desserts, particularly ice cream, or as a flavouring for cake icing. They are made from vegetable oils, sugar and dried milk.

Handling Chocolate

Storage Store chocolate products in a cool place, preferably below 25 C, 75 F but not in the refrigerator. When chocolate is kept at higher temperatures, the cocoa butter begins to melt and the surface of the chocolate becomes grey. This is known as *bloom*. It doesn't affect the flavour but it has an unappetising appearance. Keep chocolate in a dry place. Any moisture that seeps inside the package is likely to change the chocolate's texture.

Cooking Chocolate, even when combined with other ingredients, scorches easily. Use low or moderate heat when cooking a chocolate mixture on top of the stove. It is a good idea to stir the mixture while it is cooking to keep it well mixed and to avoid scorching. When making confectionery do not stir chocolate mixtures that are cooking unless instructed to do so by the recipe.

Decorating with Chocolate

A Chocolate Spiderweb Design is an unusual but easy-to-make decoration for the top of a cake. First ice a 2- or 3-layer cake with your favourite white icing. Let the cake stand until the icing is firm. Melt chocolate and let it stand until it is almost cool but not set. Spoon the cooled melted chocolate into a piping bag fitted with a small plain nozzle. Pipe the chocolate through the pastry tube, making 5 or 6 circles around the top of the cake. Immediately pull the blunt edge of a table knife across the chocolate circles from the centre to the outer edge. Do this 8 to 10 times across the top of the cake.

Chocolate Curls are not difficult to make but the temperature of the chocolate is important. It should be slightly warm so the curls will not crack, but not warm enough to melt. Unwrap the chocolate. Place it on foil or waxed paper. Let plain or milk chocolate stand 15 to 20 minutes at about 30 C, 90 F. Milk chocolate should stand at a slightly lower temperature. Use a gas oven with a pilot light or an electric oven that has been warmed slightly then turned off. Thinly shave the chocolate with a swivel-bladed vegetable peeler. Long strokes, with the peeler going diagonally across the smooth side of the chocolate, produce larger, longer curls. Carefully insert a cocktail stick or a small skewer into the curl to pick it up and place it on the dessert.

Grated Chocolate is an easy and fast way to decorate a pie, custard or cake. Most graters have two grating sections, one finer than the other. Use the size most flattering to the dish you are decorating.

Even if you only need to grate a small amount of chocolate, a large, thick piece is easier to grate than a small, thin piece. For easy cleaning-up, hold the grater on aluminium foil or waxed paper. With the grater at an angle, rub the chocolate across it.

To grate larger amounts, hold the chocolate with a paper towel so the heat of your hand doesn't melt it. A *mouli* grater is faster and more convenient than hand grating, and the chocolate is grated uniformly. You can grate chocolate in a blender if you cut it into small chunks first. However, the pieces will not be uniform in size and the friction of the blades is likely to melt the chocolate.

Decorative Chocolate Cut-outs make effective seasonal designs. Line a baking tray with aluminium foil. Melt plain chocolate pieces; pour onto the foil-lined baking tray. Cool until almost set. Cut into desired designs. Use biscuit cutters for large decorations, aspic or canapé cutters for small designs, or outline you own with the point of a sharp knife. Do not remove cut-outs from the tray. Return the tray to cool a place until the chocolate is firm. Insert a spatula under each cut-out and remove from the tray. Use as decorations for pies or cakes.

Chocolate Leaves are easy to make. Wash an assortment of leaves from non-poisonous plants such as roses or geraniums. Pat dry with paper towels. Melt plain chocolate or a combination of milk and plain chocolate, broken into pieces. With a narrow spatula or knife, spread a layer of melted chocolate about 5 mm/⅛ in thick on the *back* of each leaf just to the edge. Try not to let

Decorative Chocolate Cut-outs

any chocolate spill over to the front side of leaf. Place on a flat board or tray. Chill until firm. Carefully peel off leaves. Use them to decorate cakes or other desserts.

Drizzled Chocolate is another easy way to dress up a layer cake or a sponge cake. First, ice the cake with your favourite white icing. Swirl the sides and the top with a spatula. Let the cake stand until the icing is firm. Melt 25 g/1 oz chocolate with ½ teaspoon of lard. Cool slightly. Drizzle the melted mixture from the tip of a teaspoon around the top edge of the iced cake. Some of the chocolate will drip down the sides of the cake.

Grated Chocolate

Chocolate leaves

Cakes

Cakes have always been associated with celebrations and special occasions. We bake heart-shaped cakes for St Valentines Day, honour Mum on Mother's Day with a cake, pack a cake for a special picnic, and bake a variety of cakes for the holidays. And who wants to celebrate a birthday without a cake?

To help you with all your celebrations, or to make any day special, we have assembled a super collection of chocolate cakes. We've included cherished recipes handed down from one generation to another and in many cases we have developed streamlined versions of these classics.

Here are some hints to help you bake the perfect cake. First, assemble all the ingredients before you begin mixing. Butter or margarine will cream easier if brought to room temperature. In an effort to save time, effort and washing up, we have avoided the extra step of sifting flour wherever possible. There are a few exceptions when you are making cakes that are very delicate in texture. To measure flour, use a spoon to scoop it out of the bag or canister. Never pack flour in the measuring cup. To make a level measurement, pull the blunt edge of a straight knife across the top of the cup. If the dry ingredients are combined before being mixed into the batter, you can cut down on washing up by using a sheet of foil or waxed paper instead of an additional bowl.

Instead of repeating the various ways to tell when a cake is done in each recipe, we suggest you try one or more of the following tests. Your cake is done:

- If it has shrunk away from the sides of the pan.
- If you lightly touch the centre of the cake and the top springs back leaving no imprint of your finger.
- If a cocktail stick or skewer inserted into the centre of the cake comes out clean.

Best Fudge Cake

75 g/3 oz plain chocolate
100 g/4 oz butter or margarine
275 g/10 oz demerara or soft brown sugar
3 eggs
1 teaspoon vanilla essence
2 teaspoons bicarbonate of soda
½ teaspoon salt
275 g/10 oz plain flour
300 ml/½ pint soured cream
300 ml/½ pint boiling water

Melt the chocolate and set it aside. Grease and flour two 23-cm/9-in cake tins; set aside. Set the oven at 180 C, 350 F, gas 4. In a large bowl, cream the butter or margarine until smooth. Add the brown sugar and eggs. Beat with an electric mixer on high speed until light and fluffy, about 5 minutes. With mixer on low speed, beat in the vanilla and melted chocolate, then the bicarbonate of soda and salt. Add flour alternately with soured cream, beating on low speed until smooth. Pour in the boiling water; stir with a spoon until blended. Pour into the prepared tins. Bake for 35 minutes or until done. Cool in their tins for 10 minutes. Turn out on wire racks and leave to cool completely. Ice, if desired. **Makes one 2-layer, 23-cm/9-in cake.**

Best Cocoa Cake

225 g/8 oz butter or margarine
275 g/10 oz demerara or soft brown sugar
4 eggs
2 teaspoons vanilla essence
50 g/2 oz unsweetened cocoa powder
2 teaspoons bicarbonate of soda
½ teaspoon salt
350 g/12 oz plain flour
300 ml/½ pint soured cream

Grease and flour three 23-cm/9-in cake tins; set aside. Set the oven at 180 C, 350 F, gas 4. In a large bowl, cream the butter or margarine until smooth. Add the brown sugar and eggs. Beat with the electric mixer on high speed until light and fluffy, about 5 minutes. With the mixer on low speed, beat in the vanilla, cocoa powder, bicarbonate of soda and salt. Add the flour alternately with soured cream, beating on low speed until smooth. Pour into the prepared tins. Bake for 35 minutes or until done. Cool in the tins for 10 minutes, then turn out on wire racks and cool completely. Ice if desired. **Makes one 3-layer, 23-cm/9-in cake.**

One-bowl Chocolate Cake

100 g/4 oz plain chocolate
450 g/1 lb sifted plain flour
350 g/12 oz sugar
1 teaspoon bicarbonate of soda
1 teaspoon salt
½ teaspoon baking powder
150 ml/¼ pint water
150 ml/¼ pint buttermilk
100 g/4 oz soft margarine
2 eggs

Melt the chocolate and set it aside. Grease and flour two 23-cm/9-in cake tins; set aside. Set the oven at 180 C, 350 F, gas 4. Combine all the ingredients in a large bowl. Beat with the electric mixer on low speed for 30 seconds, then on high speed for 3 minutes. Pour into the prepared tins. Bake for 30 to 35 minutes or until done. Cool in the tins for 5 minutes. Turn out on wire racks. Cool completely. Ice, if desired. **Makes one 2-layer, 23-cm/9-in cake.**

Devilish Cake

This rich, dark-coloured cake is especially good with Glossy Icing (page 33).

100 g/4 oz plain chocolate
275 g/10 oz plain flour
225 g/8 oz granulated sugar
100 g/4 oz demerara or soft brown sugar
1 teaspoon baking soda
½ teaspoon salt
300 ml/½ pint creamy milk
100 g/4 oz butter or margarine
2 eggs
1 teaspoon vanilla essence

Melt the chocolate; set aside. Grease and flour two 23-cm/9-in cake tins; set aside. Set the oven at 180 C, 350 F, gas 4. Combine all the ingredients in a large bowl. Beat with the electric mixer on low speed for 30 seconds, then on high speed for 3 minutes. Pour into the prepared tins. Bake for 30 to 35 minutes or until done. Cool in the tins for 10 minutes. Turn out onto wire cooling racks. Cool completely. Ice, if desired. **Makes one 2-layer, 23-cm/9-in cake.**

Surprise Cupcakes

Use large muffin tins at least 6 cm/2½ in across. Or put extra mixture in lined custard cups.

225 g/8 oz cream cheese, at room temperature
50 g/2 oz sugar
1 egg
175 g/6 oz plain chocolate drops
500 g/18 oz vanilla or lemon cake mix
liquid according to directions on the packet
eggs according to directions on the packet

Line 24 muffin tins with fluted paper baking cases; set aside. Set the oven at 180 C, 350 F, gas 4. In a medium-sized bowl, beat the cream cheese with the sugar and egg until smooth. Stir in the chocolate drops and set aside. Prepare the cake mix according to the directions on the packet and fill the prepared muffin cups two-thirds full with cake mixture. Drop a heaped teaspoon of cream cheese mixture into the centre of each, the cups will be almost full. Bake for 15 to 20 minutes or until done. **Makes 24 large cupcakes.**

Old-fashioned Chocolate Cake

Milk Chocolate Icing (page 33) enhances the delicate flavour of this cake.

175 g/6 oz butter or margarine
225 g/8 oz sugar
3 egg yolks
1 teaspoon vanilla essence
275 g/10 oz sifted plain flour
40 g/1½ oz unsweetened cocoa powder
2 teaspoons baking powder
300 ml/½ pint cold water
3 egg whites

Grease and flour two 23-cm/9-in cake tins; set aside. Set the oven at 180 C, 350 F, gas 4. In a large bowl, cream the butter or margarine. Gradually add the sugar, creaming until light and fluffy. Add the egg yolks one at a time, beating well after each addition. Beat in the vanilla. Combine the flour, cocoa and baking powder. Add to the creamed mixture alternately with water, beating after each addition until smooth. In a small bowl, whisk the egg whites until stiff but not dry then gently fold them into the cake mixture. Pour into the prepared tins. Bake for about 25 minutes or until done. Cool in the tins for 10 minutes, then turn out on wire racks and cool completely. Ice, if desired. **Makes one 2-layer, 23-cm/9-in cake.**

Yule Log

Our version of the traditional Bûche Noël is time-consuming but worth it.

5 egg yolks
275 g/10 oz sugar
½ teaspoon vanilla essence
5 egg whites
175 g/6 oz sifted self-raising flour
¾ teaspoon baking powder
¼ teaspoon salt
icing sugar
Buttercream Filling
Meringue Mushrooms, page 106
BUTTERCREAM FILLING
50 g/2 oz plain chocolate
225 g/8 oz sugar
100 ml/4 fl oz water
3 egg yolks
100 g/4 oz butter, softened
1 tablespoon rum

Grease a 38 × 25 cm/15 × 10 in baking tin and line it with waxed paper. Grease the waxed paper and set it aside. Grease 2 custard cups and set them aside also. Set the oven at 190 C, 375 F, gas 5. In a small bowl, beat the egg yolks until thickened and pale yellow in colour. Gradually add 175 g/6 oz of the sugar, beating constantly. Stir in the vanilla. In a large bowl, beat the egg whites until foamy. Gradually add the rest of the sugar, beating until stiff but not dry. Fold the egg yolk mixture into the beaten egg whites. Sift together the flour, baking powder and salt and fold it into the egg mixture. Spoon about 2 tablespoons batter into each prepared custard cup. Gently spread the remaining batter in the prepared tin and bake for 10 to 12 minutes. Sprinkle icing sugar on a clean, dry tea towel. When the cake is done, loosen the edges and immediately invert onto the prepared towel. Remove the tin and waxed paper. Starting with the longer edge of cake, roll up cake and towel together. Cool. Remove the cake from the custard cups; cool. Prepare the Buttercream Filling. Unroll the cake and remove the towel. Spread the cake with half the filling. Reroll the cake without the towel and ice with the remaining filling. Lightly press both cakes from the custard cups into the filling along the side of the log to resemble knots. Spread the filling over all. Swirl with a spatula or score with a fork to resemble bark. Slice and serve. Decorate with Meringue Mushrooms. **Serves 10 to 12.**

Buttercream Filling

Melt the chocolate and set it aside to cool. In a small saucepan, bring the sugar and water to a boil. Cook to 115 C, 240 F on a sugar thermometer or soft-ball stage. Remove from the heat. While the caramel is cooking, beat the egg yolks in a small bowl until thickened and pale yellow in colour. Very gradually add the hot syrup, beating constantly. Continue beating until lukewarm. Beat in the butter 1 tablespoon at a time. Mix in the melted chocolate and rum. Beat until thickened.

Chocolate Soufflé Roll

5 eggs, separated
225 g/8 oz icing sugar
1 teaspoon vanilla essence
3 tablespoons unsweetened cocoa powder
1 tablespoon flour
300 ml/½ pint whipping or double cream
50 g/2 oz finely crushed chocolate peppermint sticks
icing sugar

Grease a 38 × 25-cm/15 × 10-in Swiss roll tin and line it with greaseproof paper. Grease this and set aside. Set the oven at 180 C, 350 F, gas 4. In a small bowl, beat the egg yolks until very thick and lemon-coloured, 5 to 6 minutes. Gradually add the icing sugar, beating until the mixture is thick again. Mix in the vanilla and cocoa. In a large bowl, beat the egg whites until stiff but not dry and carefully fold them into the egg yolk mixture. Spoon into the prepared tin and spread gently and evenly. Bake for 18 to 20 minutes or until done. Sprinkle a clean, dry tea towel with icing sugar and, when the cake is done, remove from the oven and immediately loosen the sides. Invert onto the prepared towel and remove the greaseproof paper. Starting with the shorter edge, roll up towel and cake together. Cool the rolled up cake on a wire rack and, when it is cool, whip the cream. Unroll the cake, remove the towel and spread the cake with whipped cream. Sprinkle with crushed chocolate peppermint sticks. Roll up the cake like a Swiss roll and sprinkle with icing sugar. **Serves 8.**

Banana and Nut Cake

The perfect cake for a picnic.

150 g/5 oz butter or margarine
225 g/8 oz sugar
2 eggs
1 teaspoon vanilla essence
225 g/8 oz plain flour
1 teaspoon baking powder
1 teaspoon bicarbonate of soda
½ teaspoon salt
2 tablespoons unsweetened cocoa powder
300 ml/½ pint soured cream
2 large ripe bananas, mashed
100 g/4 oz chopped nuts

Grease a 33 × 23-cm/13 × 9-in baking tin and set it aside. Set the oven at 180 C, 350 F, gas 4. In a large bowl, beat the butter or margarine and sugar until light and fluffy. Beat in the eggs 1 at a time, and the vanilla essence. Combine the flour, baking powder, bicarbonate of soda, salt and cocoa. Beat alternately with the soured cream into the creamed mixture. Stir in the bananas and nuts. Pour into the prepared tin and bake for 35 to 40 minutes or until done. Cool in the tin. **Makes one single-layer, 33 × 23-cm/13 × 9-in cake.**

Mocha Cake

100 g/4 oz butter or margarine
175 g/6 oz demerara or soft brown sugar
3 egg yolks
1 teaspoon vanilla essence
350 g/12 oz plain flour
40 g/1½ oz unsweetened cocoa powder
1½ teaspoons bicarbonate of soda
½ teaspoon salt
350 ml/12 fl oz cold strong coffee
3 egg whites
150 g/5 oz granulated sugar

Grease and flour two 23-cm/9-in cake tins; set aside. Set the oven at 180 C, 350 F, gas 4. In a large bowl, cream the butter or margarine and sugar until light and fluffy. Add the egg yolks one at a time, beating well after each addition. Stir in the vanilla essence. Sift together the flour, cocoa, bicarbonate of soda and salt. Add to the creamed mixture alternately with coffee, beating well after each addition. In a medium bowl, beat the egg whites until soft peaks form. Gradually add the granulated sugar, beating until stiff peaks form. Fold into the mixture. Pour into prepared tins. Bake for 35 to 40 minutes or until done. Cool in the tins for 10 minutes then turn out on wire racks and cool completely, then ice. **Makes one 2-layer, 23-cm/9-in cake.**

Velvet Cake

100 g/4 oz butter or margarine
275 g/10 oz sugar
2 eggs
½ teaspoon salt
275 g/10 oz plain flour
175 ml/6 fl oz creamy milk
3 tablespoons unsweetened cocoa powder
1 teaspoon vanilla essence
1 teaspoon baking soda
1 teaspoon vinegar
vanilla icing (see below)
VANILLA ICING
40 g/1½ oz flour
300 ml/½ pint milk
225 g/8 oz sugar
225 g/8 oz butter or margarine
1 teaspoon vanilla essence

Lightly grease and flour two 23-cm/9-in cake tins; set aside. Set the oven at 180 C, 350 F, gas 4. In a large bowl cream the butter or margarine and sugar. Beat in the eggs until light and fluffy. Add salt. Beat in the flour and cocoa alternately with milk. Mix the vanilla essence, bicarbonate of soda and vinegar in a small bowl. Sprinkle over the mixture and stir in. Pour into prepared tins. Bake for 30 to 35 minutes or until done. Cool in the tins for 10 minutes. Turn out on wire racks and cool completely. Prepare the Vanilla Icing. Ice between the layers, then the sides and top of the cake. **Makes one 2-layer, 23-cm/9-in cake.**

Vanilla Icing

Combine the flour and milk in a small saucepan. Beat with a whisk until smooth. Stir constantly over low heat until thickened. Cool. In a medium bowl, cream the sugar and butter or margarine. Add the vanilla. Beat in the cooled flour-milk mixture until the icing is fluffy and resembles whipped cream.

German Sweet Chocolate Cake

Here is the authentic recipe for this famous cake.

150 g/6 oz plain chocolate
150 ml/¼ pint boiling water
225 g/8 oz butter or margarine
275 g/10 oz sugar
4 egg yolks
1 teaspoon vanilla essence
400 g/14 oz plain flour
1 teaspoon bicarbonate of soda
½ teaspoon salt
300 ml/½ pint creamy milk
4 egg whites, stiffly beaten
Coconut and Almond Icing (see below)
COCONUT AND ALMOND ICING
300 ml/½ pint evaporated milk
225 g/8 oz sugar
3 egg yolks, lightly beaten
100 g/4 oz butter or margarine
1 teaspoon vanilla essence
225 g/8 oz desiccated coconut
100 g/4 oz chopped almonds

Melt the chocolate over boiling water and set it aside to cool. Line the base of three 20- or 23-cm/8- or 9-in cake tins with greaseproof paper; set aside. Set the oven at 180 C, 350 F, gas 4. Cream the butter or margarine and sugar until fluffy. Add the egg yolks one at a time, beating well after each. Blend in the vanilla and chocolate mixture. Sift together the flour, bicarbonate of soda and salt. Add alternately with the creamy milk to the chocolate mixture, beating after each addition until smooth. Fold in the beaten egg whites. Pour into the prepared tins. Bake for 30 to 40 minutes. Cool in their tins for 10 minutes then turn out on wire racks and cool completely. Prepare the Coconut and Almond Icing. Ice only the top of each layer. **Makes one 3-layer, 20- or 23-cm/8- or 9-in cake.**

Coconut and Almond Icing

Combine evaporated milk, sugar, egg yolks, butter or margarine and vanilla in a medium saucepan. Stir over medium heat until thickened, about 12 minutes. Stir in coconut and almonds. Cool, beating occasionally, until thick enough to spread.

Peanut Butter Streusel Cake

Ideal for lunch boxes or picnics.

350 g/12 oz flour
350 g/12 oz demerara or soft brown sugar
175 g/6 oz crunchy peanut butter
100 g/4 oz butter or margarine
3 eggs
1 teaspoon baking powder
½ teaspoon bicarbonate of soda
150 ml/¼ pint milk
1 teaspoon vanilla essence
75 g/3 oz plain chocolate drops
Chocolate Glaze (see below)
chopped peanuts, if desired
CHOCOLATE GLAZE
2 tablespoons butter or margarine
75 g/3 oz plain chocolate, broken into pieces
2 tablespoons milk
100 g/4 oz sifted icing sugar

Grease and flour a 33 × 23-cm/13 × 9-in baking tin; set aside. Set the oven at 180 C, 350 F, gas 4. In a large bowl, combine the flour and sugar. Mix in the peanut butter and butter or margarine until the mixture is crumbly. Remove about ¼ of the mixture and set aside. To the remaining mixture, add the eggs, baking powder, bicarbonate of soda, milk and vanilla. Beat with an electric mixer on medium speed for about 3 minutes. Spoon half of the mixture into the prepared tin. Sprinkle with the reserved peanut butter mixture, then with chocolate drops. Top with the other half of the cake batter. Bake for 30 to 35 minutes or until done. Cool in the tin. Prepare the Chocolate Glaze and spread on the cooled cake. Sprinkle with peanuts, if desired. **Makes one single-layer, 33 × 23-cm/13 × 9-in cake.**

Chocolate Glaze

In a small saucepan, combine the butter or margarine with the chocolate pieces and milk. Cook over low heat until the chocolate melts. Remove from the heat and stir in the icing sugar.

Mississippi Mud Cake

4 eggs
400 g/14 oz sugar
225 g/8 oz butter or margarine, melted
225 g/8 oz plain flour
40 g/1½ oz unsweetened cocoa powder
1 teaspoon vanilla essence
75 g/3 oz desiccated coconut
50 g/2 oz chopped cashew nuts
½ quantity Marshmallow Frosting (page 36)
using white marshmallows only
Levée Frosting (see below)
100 g/4 oz chopped nuts, if desired
LEVEE FROSTING
100 g/4 oz butter or margarine, melted
25 g/1 oz unsweetened cocoa powder
1 teaspoon vanilla essence
6 tablespoons milk

Grease and flour a 33 × 23-cm/13 × 9-in baking tin; set aside. Set the oven at 180 C, 350 F, gas 4. In a large bowl, beat the eggs until thick. Gradually beat in the sugar. Combine the melted butter or margarine with the flour, cocoa, vanilla, coconut and cashew nuts. Add to the egg-sugar mixture and stir well with a spoon. Pour into the prepared tin and bake for 30 minutes or until done. Remove from the oven. Immediately spread the Marshmallow Frosting gently over the surface of the cake. Prepare the Levée Frosting and spread it gently over the warm Marshmallow Frosting, swirling to give a marbled effect. Sprinkle nuts over the top, if desired. **Makes one single-layer 33 × 23-cm/13 × 9-in cake.**

Levee Frosting

Blend all the ingredients in a medium-sized bowl.

How to make Mississippi Mud Cake

1 As soon as you take the cake out of the oven, spread with the marshmallow frosting. Heat from the freshly baked cake will soften the marshmallow.

2 While the marshmallow frosting is still warm, gently spread it over the top. Then pull a spatula through both marshmallow and frosting to make a marbled effect.

Black Forest Cake

6 eggs
175 g/6 oz sugar
1 teaspoon vanilla essence
75 g/3 oz plain flour
50 g/2 oz unsweetened cocoa powder
75 g/3 oz butter or margarine, melted
Brandied Syrup (see below)
600 ml/1 pint whipping cream
25 g/1 oz icing sugar
1 (425-g/15-oz) can sweet, dark stoneless cherries,
drained
25 g/1 oz plain or milk chocolate
BRANDIED SYRUP
175 g/6 oz sugar
300 ml/½ pint cold water
3 tablespoons kirsch or Cointreau

Grease and flour three 20-cm/8-in cake tins; set aside. Set the oven at 180 C, 350 F, gas 4. In a large bowl, beat the eggs until light and fluffy. Add the sugar and vanilla and beat at high speed until thick, about 5 minutes. Combine the flour and cocoa and gradually sift over the egg mixture while very gently folding in. Stir in the melted butter or margarine 2 tablespoons at a time until just blended, then spoon the mixture into the prepared tins. Bake for 15 to 20 minutes or until done. Cool in the tin for 5 minutes then turn out onto wire racks and leave to cool completely.

Prepare the Brandied Syrup. With a fork, prick each cake layer 12 to 14 times and carefully spoon syrup over each layer. Whip the cream until it begins to thicken, add the icing sugar and continue beating until stiff. Place 1 cake layer on a serving plate and spread with whipped cream, top with the second layer and spread also with whipped cream. Place the third layer on top and arrange the cherries on this, leaving about 1 cm/½ in around the edge for whipped cream. Spread the sides and outer edge of the top with the remaining whipped cream then refrigerate the cake. Make chocolate curls or grate chocolate with the coarse side of a grater and gently press them into the whipped cream. Refrigerate until needed. **Makes one 3-layer, 20-cm/8-in cake.**

Brandied Syrup

In a small saucepan, bring the sugar and water to a boil, stirring until the sugar dissolves. Continue boiling without stirring for 5 minutes. Remove from the heat and cool to lukewarm. Finally, stir in the kirsch or Cointreau.

Spicy Fruitcake

Mellow this cake for a few weeks in a brandy- or juice-soaked cloth inside a foil wrapping.

25 g/1 oz plain chocolate
100 g/4 oz currants
450 g/1 lb raisins
100 g/4 oz chopped mixed peel
100 g/4 oz chopped cashew nuts
100 g/4 oz flaked almonds
275 g/10 oz plain flour
1 teaspoon nutmeg
1 teaspoon cinnamon
1 teaspoon ground cloves
½ teaspoon bicarbonate of soda
225 g/8 oz soft margarine
225 g/8 oz demerara or soft brown sugar
6 eggs, separated
3 tablespoons lemon juice
3 tablespoons orange juice

Melt the chocolate and set it aside. Grease the bottom and sides of a 25-cm/10-in, deep ring mould and line it with greaseproof paper or aluminium foil; set aside. Set the oven at 150 C, 300 F, gas 2. In a large bowl, thoroughly mix the currants, raisins, chopped peel, nuts and half the flour. Combine the remaining flour, nutmeg, cinnamon, cloves and bicarbonate of soda in a small bowl; set aside. In a large bowl, cream the soft margarine and brown sugar until light and fluffy. Add the egg yolks one at a time, beating well after each addition. With the electric mixer on low speed, blend in the melted chocolate. Alternately beat in the flour-spice mixture and the fruit juices, beating after each addition until just smooth. Stir into the fruit-nut mixture. Beat the egg whites until stiff and fold them into the batter. Turn into the prepared tin. Bake for 2 hours and 20 minutes or until done. Cool completely in the tin. **Makes one 25-cm/10-in cake.**

Chocolate Fruitcake

100 g/4 oz plain chocolate
100 g/4 oz soft margarine
225 g/8 oz sugar
3 eggs
275 g/10 oz plain flour
2 teaspoons baking powder
1 teaspoon salt
1 teaspoon cinnamon
5 tablespoons milk
450 g/1 lb chopped mixed peel
275 g/10 oz raisins
100 g/4 oz chopped nuts
1 tablespoon brandy

Grease the base and sides of a 25-cm/10-in, deep ring mould and line with greaseproof paper or aluminium foil; set aside. Preheat the oven to 140 C, 275 F. Melt chocolate; set aside. In a large bowl, cream the soft margarine and sugar until fluffy. Add the eggs one at a time, beating well after each addition. Stir in the melted chocolate. Combine the flour, baking powder, salt and cinnamon and add to the chocolate mixture alternately with the milk. Stir in the chopped mixed peel, raisins, nuts and brandy. Pour into the prepared tin and bake for 1¼–1½ hours or until done. Cool in the tin for 10 minutes. Turn out onto a wire rack. **Makes one 25-cm/10-in cake.**

Date Cake

A versatile dessert: serve it warm or cold, plain or with ice cream.

225 g/8 oz chopped dates
1 teaspoon grated orange peel
1 teaspoon bicarbonate of soda
450 ml/¾ pint boiling water
175 g/6 oz butter or margarine, softened
225 g/8 oz sugar
1 egg
225 g/8 oz flour
2 teaspoons baking powder
½ teaspoon salt
WALNUT TOPPING
100 g/4 oz sugar
50 g/2 oz chopped walnuts
175 g/6 oz plain chocolate drops

Grease a 33 × 23-cm/13 × 9-in baking tin; set aside. Set the oven at 180 C, 350 F, gas 4. In a small bowl, combine the dates, orange peel and baking soda. Pour over the boiling water and set aside. In a large bowl, cream the butter or margarine and sugar until light and fluffy. Beat in the egg. Combine the flour, baking powder and salt and add alternately with the date mixture to the creamed mixture. Stir until blended and pour into the prepared tin. Prepare the Walnut Topping and sprinkle over the mixture in the tin. Bake for about 1 hour or until done.

Walnut Topping

Mix all the ingredients in a small bowl.

Cherry-chocolate Cake

25 g/1 oz plain chocolate
275 g/10 oz plain flour
175 g/6 oz sugar
1 teaspoon bicarbonate of soda
$\frac{1}{4}$ teaspoon salt
100 g/4 oz soft margarine
150 ml/$\frac{1}{4}$ pint milk
3 tablespoons maraschino cherry juice
2 eggs
75 g/3 oz chopped maraschino cherries
Cherry-chocolate Icing (see below)
CHERRY-CHOCOLATE ICING
25 g/1 oz plain chocolate
100 g/4 oz butter or margarine
350 g/12 oz sifted icing sugar
2 tablespoons maraschino cherry juice
75 g/3 oz chopped maraschino cherries

Grease and flour two 23-cm/9-in cake tins and set them aside. Set the oven at 180 C, 350 F, gas 4. Melt the chocolate and set aside also. In a large bowl, combine the flour, sugar, bicarbonate of soda and salt. Make a well in the centre of the flour mixture. Drop in the butter or margarine, milk, cherry juice and eggs. Blend with the electric mixer on low speed, then beat on medium speed for 2 minutes. Add the melted chocolate and cherries and beat for another minute. Pour into the prepared tins and bake for 25 to 30 minutes or until done. Cool in their tins for 10 minutes, then turn out onto wire racks. Cool completely. Finally, prepare the Cherry-chocolate Icing and spread it over the top. **Makes one 2-layer, 23-cm/9-in cake.**

Cherry-chocolate Icing

Melt the chocolate; set aside. In a small bowl, cream the butter or margarine, then add the icing sugar and cherry juice and beat until smooth. Stir in the melted chocolate and cherries.

Peachy Cream Cake

100 g/4 oz almond paste
3 egg yolks
50 g/2 oz butter or margarine
50 g/2 oz plain flour
1 teaspoon baking powder
100 g/4 oz chocolate spread
3 egg whites
1 (410-g/14$\frac{1}{2}$-oz) can peach slices
300 ml/$\frac{1}{2}$ pint whipping cream
50 g/2 oz halved maraschino cherries

Grease and flour two 18-cm/7-in cake tins; set aside. Set the oven at 180 C, 350 F, gas 4. In a large bowl, mix the almond paste, egg yolks and butter or margarine. Beat until light. Mix in the flour and baking powder, then add the chocolate spread. In a small mixing bowl, beat the egg whites until stiff. Fold into the chocolate mixture. Divide the mixture between the two tins. Bake for 12 to 15 minutes or until done. Cool in the tins. Drain the peaches, reserving 75 ml/2$\frac{1}{2}$ fl oz syrup. In a small bowl, whip the cream and reserved peach syrup until soft peaks form. Spread on the cooled cake. Top with the drained peaches and maraschino cherries. **Makes one double-layer, 18-cm/7-in cake.**

Overleaf **Peachy Cream Cake**

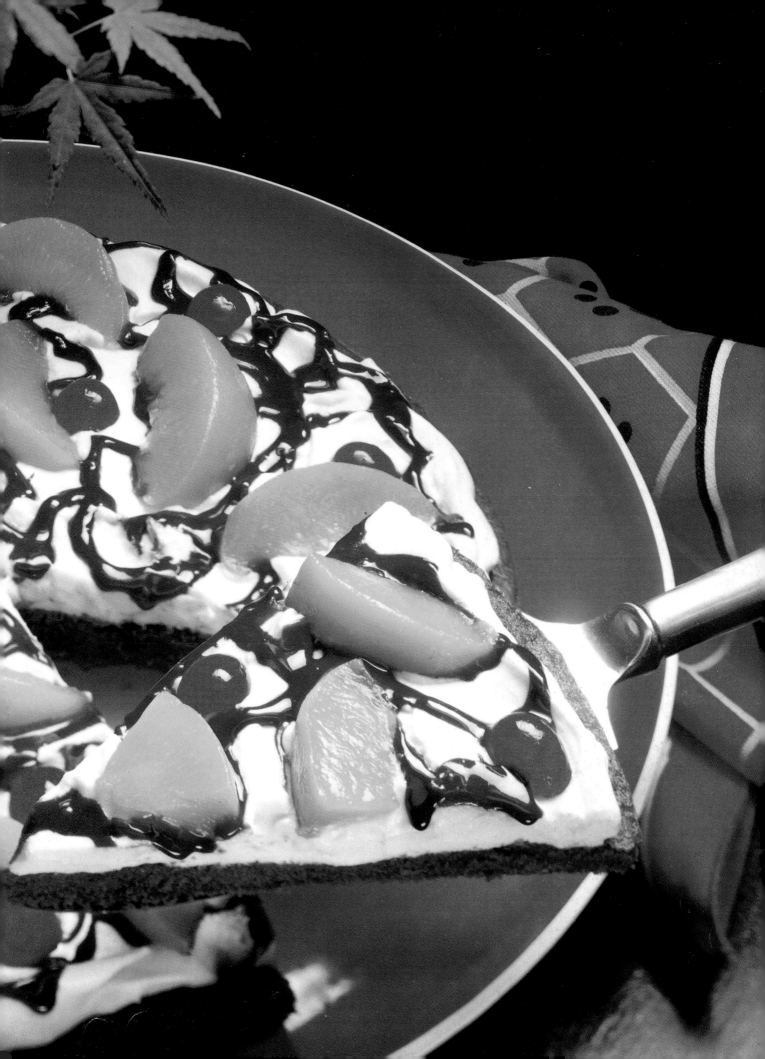

Cocoa Chiffon Cake

225 g/8 oz plain flour
100 g/4 oz sugar
40 g/1½ oz unsweetened cocoa powder
3 teaspoons baking powder
1 teaspoon salt
8 tablespoons cooking oil
4 tablespoons milk
7 eggs separated
150 ml/¼ pint cold water
1 teaspoon vanilla essence
½ teaspoon cream of tartar
Creamy Glaze (see below)
CREAMY GLAZE
25 g/1 oz butter or margarine
225 g/8 oz sifted icing sugar
1 teaspoon vanilla essence
2 tablespoons hot water

Set the oven at 160 C, 325 F, gas 3. In a large bowl, combine the flour, sugar, cocoa, baking powder and salt. Make a well in the mixture and add the oil, milk, egg yolks, water and vanilla essence. Beat until smooth. In another large bowl, beat the egg whites and cream of tartar until very stiff peaks form. Gradually pour the mixture over the beaten whites, gently folding until just blended. Spoon into an ungreased 25-cm/10-in, deep ring mould. Bake for 1 to 1¼ hours or until done. Invert the tin onto a wire rack and let it stand upside down until completely cool. Prepare the Creamy Glaze and spoon over the top of the cake, letting the excess drip down the sides. **Makes one 25-cm/10-in cake.**

Creamy Glaze

In a small saucepan, melt the butter or margarine. Remove from the heat, stir in the icing sugar and vanilla, then add the water. Mix until smooth.

Chocolate Chip Chiffon Cake

75 g/3 oz sweet baking chocolate (Kake-Brand)
275 g/10 oz plain flour
225 g/8 oz sugar
3 teaspoons baking powder
½ teaspoon salt
6 tablespoons cooking oil
7 eggs, separated
150 ml/¼ pint cold water
2 teaspoons vanilla essence
½ teaspoon cream of tartar
Sweet Chocolate Glaze (see below)
SWEET CHOCOLATE GLAZE
50 g/2 oz cooking chocolate
2 tablespoons butter or margarine
100 g/4 oz icing sugar
½ teaspoon vanilla essence
2 tablespoons hot water

Grate the chocolate and set it aside. Set the oven at 160 C, 325 F, gas 3. In a large bowl, combine the flour, sugar, baking powder and salt. Make a well in the mixture and add the oil, egg yolks, water and vanilla. Beat until smooth. Gently stir in the grated chocolate. In another large bowl, beat the egg whites until foamy. Add the cream of tartar and beat until very stiff peaks form. Gradually pour this mixture into the beaten whites, folding until just blended. Pour into an ungreased, 25-cm/10-in, deep ring mould. Bake for 1–1¼ hours or until done. Invert the tin onto a wire cooling rack and let stand upside down until completely cool. Finally, prepare the Sweet Chocolate Glaze and spoon it over the cooled cake, letting the excess drip down the sides. **Makes one 25-cm/10-in cake.**

Sweet Chocolate Glaze

In a small saucepan over low heat, melt the chocolate and butter or margarine. Remove from the heat and stir in the icing sugar, vanilla and hot water.

Cinnamon Chiffon Cake

100 g/4 oz plain chocolate
250 g/9 oz sugar
400 g/14 oz sifted plain flour
½ teaspoon salt
1 teaspoon baking powder
1 teaspoon cinnamon
4 tablespoons cooking oil
300 ml/½ pint milk
2 eggs, separated

Melt the chocolate and set it aside. Grease and flour two 23-cm/9-in cake tins; set aside. Set the oven at 180 C, 350 F, gas 4. In a large bowl, combine 175 g/6 oz of the sugar, the flour, salt, baking powder and cinnamon. Add the oil, milk and egg yolks and beat until smooth. Stir in the melted chocolate. In a small bowl, beat the egg whites until foamy. Gradually add the remaining sugar, beating until very stiff peaks form. Gently fold the beaten egg whites into the chocolate mixture. Pour into the prepared tins and bake for 30 to 35 minutes or until done. Cool the tins for 10 minutes then turn out onto wire racks. Cool completely. Ice if desired. **Makes one 2-layer, 23-cm/9-in cake.**

Cinnamon Pound Cake

225 g/8 oz butter
350 g/12 oz sugar
4 eggs
350 g/12 oz plain flour
½ teaspoon baking powder
½ teaspoon bicarbonate of soda
50 g/2 oz unsweetened cocoa powder
1 teaspoon cinnamon
300 ml/½ pint soured cream
1 teaspoon vanilla essence

Grease a 25-cm/10-in ring mould and set it aside. Set the oven at 160 C, 325 F, gas 3. In a large bowl, cream the butter and sugar until smooth. Add the eggs one at a time, beating well after each addition. Combine the flour, baking powder, bicarbonate of soda, cocoa and cinnamon. Add alternately to the egg mixture with the soured cream, beating after each addition. Stir in the vanilla and pour into the prepared tin. Bake for 1¼ hours or until done, then cool in the tin for 10 minutes and turn out onto a wire rack. Cool completely. **Makes one 25-cm/10-in cake.**

Swirled Pound Cake

You'll love the marbled effect and superb taste.

225 g/8 oz butter
350 g/12 oz sugar
6 eggs
300 ml/½ pint soured cream
3 teaspoons baking powder
400 g/14 oz plain flour
1 teaspoon vanilla essence
3 tablespoons unsweetened cocoa powder
icing sugar or any chocolate glaze from pages 31 to 38

Grease a 23-cm/10-in ring mould and set it aside. Set the oven at 160 C, 325 F, gas 3. In a large bowl, cream the butter and sugar until light and fluffy. Add the eggs one at a time, beating well after each addition. Mix in the soured cream, baking powder, flour and vanilla. Spoon half the batter into the prepared tin and stir cocoa into the remaining batter. With a large spoon, drop the chocolate mixture evenly on top of the plain mixture. Using a palette knife or a narrow spatula, cut down into both mixtures and pull through in a zig-zag pattern to create a marbled effect. Bake for 1 hour or until done. Remove from the oven and cool in the tin for 10 minutes. Turn out onto a wire rack. When cool, sprinkle with icing sugar or drizzle with chocolate glaze. **Makes one 25-cm/10-in cake.**

Cocoa Pound Cake

Exceptionally moist and light with a mild chocolate flavour.

225 g/8 oz butter
100 g/4 oz soft margarine
400 g/14 oz sugar
5 eggs
400 g/14 oz plain flour
$\frac{1}{2}$ teaspoon baking powder
$\frac{1}{2}$ teaspoon salt
50 g/2 oz unsweetened cocoa powder
300 ml/$\frac{1}{2}$ pint milk
1 tablespoon vanilla essence

Grease thoroughly a 25-cm/10-in, deep ring mould; set aside. Set the oven at 160 c, 325 f, gas 3. In a large bowl, cream the butter, soft margarine and sugar until light and fluffy. Add the eggs one at a time, beating well after each addition. Combine the flour, baking powder, salt and cocoa and add alternately to the creamed mixture with the milk. Beat until blended. Stir in the vanilla and pour into the prepared tin. Bake for $1\frac{1}{4}$ hours or until done. Cool in the tin for 10 minutes. Turn out onto a wire rack. **Makes one 25-cm/10-in cake.**

Shortcut Sicilian Cake

1 madeira cake, approximately 20 × 7.5 cm/8 × 3 in
225 g/8 oz ricotta cheese
2 tablespoons sugar
1 tablespoon milk
2 tablespoons almond-flavoured liqueur
25 g/1 oz chopped mixed peel
2 tablespoons finely chopped toasted almonds
25 g/1 oz plain chocolate, grated
Almond-chocolate Glaze (see below)
ALMOND-CHOCOLATE GLAZE
100 g/4 oz sugar
$1\frac{1}{2}$ tablespoons cornflour
100 ml/4 fl oz water
25 g/1 oz plain chocolate, broken in chunks
1 tablespoon butter
2 teaspoons almond-flavoured liqueur

Cut the cake horizontally into 3 layers; set aside. In a medium bowl, beat the ricotta cheese, sugar, milk and liqueur until smooth. Stir in the mixed peel, almonds and grated chocolate. Spread between the cake layers but not on the top or sides. Prepare the Almond-chocolate Glaze and spread over the cake, letting the excess drip down the sides. Refrigerate until serving time. **Makes one 3-layer loaf cake.**

Almond-chocolate Glaze

In a medium sized saucepan, combine the sugar and cornflour. Stir in the water and add the chocolate. Stir constantly over medium heat until thickened. Remove from the heat. Stir in the butter and liqueur.

Marble Angel Cake

A delectable American angel-food cake with light chocolate marbling.

6 egg yolks
12 egg whites
$1\frac{1}{2}$ teaspoons cream of tartar
225 g/8 oz sugar
1 teaspoon vanilla essence
$\frac{1}{2}$ teaspoon almond extract
175 g/6 oz plain flour
$\frac{1}{4}$ teaspoon salt
2 tablespoons powdered drinking chocolate
Light and Easy Glaze (see below)
LIGHT AND EASY GLAZE
150 g/5 oz icing sugar
1 tablespoon powdered drinking chocolate
25 g/1 oz melted butter or margarine
2 tablespoons hot water

Set the oven at 190 C, 375 F, gas 5. In a small bowl, beat the egg yolks with an electric mixer on high speed until very thick and pale yellow in colour, about 5 minutes; set aside. In a large bowl, beat the egg whites until foamy, add the cream of tartar and beat until soft peaks form. Gradually add half the sugar, beating until stiff peaks form. Gently fold in the vanilla and almond essences. In a medium-sized bowl, combine the rest of the sugar, the flour and salt and sprinkle $\frac{1}{4}$ of this mixture over the beaten egg whites; gently fold in. Repeat this process until all the sugar-flour mixture is folded into the egg whtes. Pour half the egg white mixture into another large bowl and fold in the beaten egg yolks and the drinking chocolate mix. Spoon alternate layers of white and chocolate mixtures into an ungreased 25-cm/10-in angel cake mould or cake tin. Carefully cut through the mixture with a palette knife to create a marbled effect. Bake for 40 minutes or until done. Invert onto a wire cooling rack. Let stand upside down until completely cool, then remove from the mould or tin. Prepare the Light and Easy Glaze and spoon over the top of the cool cake, letting the excess drip down the sides. **Makes one 25-cm/10-in cake.**

Light and Easy Glaze

In a small bowl, combine the icing sugar and drinking chocolate mix. Add the melted butter or margarine and hot water. Mix until smooth.

How to make Marble Angel Cake

1 Create a two-toned effect by dividing beaten egg white mixture in 2 bowls. Add the drinking chocolate mix and the egg yolks to one bowl. Spoon alternate layers of light and dark mixture into the mould.

2 When all the mixture is in the mould, carefully swirl a small palette knife through it to give a marbled effect. The top will appear slightly two-toned. When you cut the baked cake, it will have a definite marbled look.

Icings, Sauces and Fillings

As you might expect in a chocolate cookbook, most of the icings you'll find here are made with some form of chocolate, but we have included a few non-chocolate icings just in case you like a contrast of flavours for chocolate cakes.

In a few of the cake recipes we suggested a specific icing that we liked with that particular cake; you may find others that you might like as well or better. Next time you make a chocolate cake, look through this icing section and choose one that seems to go well with your cake.

Did you realise that most basic chocolate or fudge sauces can be made ahead and kept covered in the refrigerator until needed? By keeping one of these on hand, you can create an impressive dessert with ice cream or plain bought cake at a moment's notice. For a quick hot fudge sundae, heat the sauce over hot water or in the microwave oven, then spoon over ice cream and top with whipped cream and grated chocolate or chopped nuts.

Black Beauty Icing

5 tablespoons evaporated milk, not diluted
75 g/3 oz sugar
25 g/1 oz butter or margarine
1 tablespoon golden syrup
175 g/6 oz plain chocolate, broken into pieces

In a medium-sized saucepan, combine the milk, sugar, butter or margarine and golden syrup. Bring to a boil, stirring constantly then lower the heat and simmer for 5 minutes. Remove from heat and immediately stir in the chocolate pieces. Beat until smooth. Cool until spreadable. This quantity will ice a 33 × 23 cm/13 × 9 in cake, or thinly ice the top and sides of one 2-layer, 20-cm/8-in cake.

Glossy Icing

This is our favourite recipe for Devilish Cake (see page 17)

25 g/1 oz butter
50 g/2 oz plain chocolate
275 g/10 oz icing sugar
$\frac{1}{4}$ teaspoon salt
3 tablespoons milk

In a medium-sized saucepan, melt the butter and chocolate over low heat. Stir in the icing sugar, salt and milk and beat until smooth. Place the saucepan in a bowl of iced water and continue beating until it reaches a spreading consistency. This quantity fills and ices one 2-layer, 20 or 23-cm/8 or 9-in cake.

Fudge Icing

50 g/2 oz butter or margarine
175 g/6 oz plain chocolate, broken into pieces
175 g/6 oz granulated sugar
5 tablespoons milk
$\frac{1}{4}$ teaspoon salt
225 g/8 oz icing sugar
1 teaspoon vanilla essence
1 to 2 tablespoons milk, if needed

In a medium-sized saucepan, combine the butter or margarine with the chocolate pieces, granulated sugar, milk and salt. Bring to a boil, stirring constantly then lower the heat and simmer for 3 minutes. Remove from the heat and stir in the icing sugar and vanilla. Beat until smooth. If the icing becomes too thick to spread, add a tablespoon or two of milk. This quantity fills and ices one 2-layer, 20 or 23-cm/8 or 9-in cake.

Milk Chocolate Icing

Cream and butter give this icing the look and taste of milk chocolate.

25 g/1 oz plain chocolate
50 g/2 oz softened butter or margarine
225 g/8 oz sifted icing sugar
1 egg yolk
$\frac{1}{2}$ teaspoon vanilla essence
About 2 tablespoons single cream

Melt the chocolate and set it aside to cool. In a medium-sized mixing bowl, cream the butter or margarine. Gradually blend in half the icing sugar. Mix in the egg yolk, melted chocolate and vanilla. Gradually beat in sugar and add enough cream to bring the icing to a spreading consistency. This quantity fills and ices one 2-layer, 20 or 23-cm/8 or 9-in cake.

Light Fudge Frosting

A mild and creamy fudge frosting

350 g/12 oz sugar
4 tablespoons golden syrup
100 ml/4 fl oz milk
100 g/4 oz margarine
50 g/2 oz plain chocolate
¼ teaspoon salt
1 teaspoon vanilla essence

Combine all the ingredients except the vanilla in a medium-sized saucepan. Stir constantly over medium heat until the chocolate melts and the sugar dissolves. Bring to a boil, stirring constantly, then boil rapidly, still stirring constantly, for 1 minute or until the mixture reaches 105 C, 220 F on a sugar thermometer. Remove from heat and stir in the vanilla. Place the pan in a bowl of iced water to cool slightly, about 5 minutes, then beat until the icing loses its gloss and is spreadable, about 10 minutes. This quantity fills and ices one 2-layer 20 or 23-cm/8 or 9-in cake.

Cocoa-butter Frosting

75 g/3 oz softened butter or margarine
25 g/1 oz unsweetened cocoa powder
225 g/8 oz sifted icing sugar
1 teaspoon vanilla essence
2 tablespoons milk

In a medium-sized bowl, cream the butter or margarine. Add the cocoa, icing sugar, vanilla and milk and beat until the icing is smooth and spreadable. This quantity fills and ices one 2-layer, 20 or 23-cm/8 or 9-in cake.

Cream Cheese Icing

A rich chocolate icing that's ideal for a large single-layer cake.

50 g/2 oz plain chocolate
75 g/3 oz cream cheese, at room temperature
2 tablespoons milk
225 g/8 oz sifted icing sugar
1 teaspoon vanilla essence

Melt the chocolate and set it aside. In a medium-sized bowl, combine the cream cheese and milk. Gradually mix in the icing sugar until smooth. Add the melted chocolate and vanilla and beat until blended. This quantity ices one 33 × 25-cm/13 × 9-in cake.

Soured Cream Icing

175 g/6 oz plain chocolate, broken into pieces
50 g/2 oz butter or margarine
150 ml/¼ pint soured cream
1 teaspoon vanilla essence
225 g/8 oz sifted icing sugar

In a medium-sized saucepan, melt the chocolate pieces and the butter or margarine and leave to cool for several minutes. Stir in the soured cream, vanilla and icing sugar. Beat until smooth. This quantity fills and ices one 2-layer, 20 or 23-cm/8 or 9-in cake.

How to Ice a Cake

1 After the layer cake has completely cooled, use your hand or a small brush to remove loose crumbs from around the sides and bottom. If these crumbs are left on the cake, they give the icing a lumpy appearance.

2 Turn the bottom layer of the cake upside down on the plate. The flat side of the cake should be on top and the round side on the bottom. Spread icing over this layer almost to the edge. If your recipe calls for a separate filling, spread the filling instead of the icing between the layers.

3 Place the second cake layer on top of icing or filling with the bottom or flat side of this layer down and the rounded side up. This is done so that the flat sides of the layers will fit together and the top will have a slight dome shape. Ice the sides of both cake layers with a thick layer of icing. If the cake is very crumbly, first cover with a very thin layer of icing to seal in the crumbs, then apply a thicker layer.

4 The last step is to ice the top of the cake. Spoon the remaining icing on the top. Spread with a palette knife to meet the icing on the side, then make swirl designs or smooth it with a spatula. Before the icing sets, sprinkle with nuts, coconut or chocolate vermicelli, if desired.

Peanut Frosting

Peanut butter frosting delicately flavoured with chocolate and sprinkled with crunchy peanuts.

50 g/2 oz plain chocolate
25 g/1 oz softened butter or margarine
25 g/1 oz peanut butter
1 teaspoon vanilla essence
225 g/8 oz icing sugar
2 tablespoons milk
chopped peanuts

Melt the chocolate and set it aside. In a medium-sized bowl, cream the butter or margarine and peanut butter. Stir in the melted chocolate and vanilla. Add the icing sugar alternately with the milk, beating until creamy and smooth. Sprinkle the top of the iced cake with chopped peanuts. This quantity fills and ices one 2-layer, 20 or 23-cm/8 or 9-in cake.

Mint Icing

This easy-to-make mint icing is a natural choice for chocolate cakes.

2 egg whites
50 g/2 oz sugar
pinch of salt
225 g/8 oz golden syrup
$\frac{1}{4}$ teaspoon peppermint essence
several drops red food colouring

In a small bowl, beat the egg whites until foamy. Gradually add the sugar and salt and beat until stiff peaks form. In a small saucepan, heat the golden syrup to boiling then slowly pour it over the beaten egg whites, beating constantly. Add the peppermint essence and food colouring. Continue beating until thick enough to spread. This quantity fills and ices one 2-layer, 20 or 23-cm/8 or 9-in cake.

Mocha Icing

50 g/2 oz softened butter or margarine
175 g/6 oz sifted icing sugar
2 tablespoons unsweetened cocoa powder
1 teaspoon vanilla essence
1 tablespoon hot strong coffee

In a medium-sized bowl, cream the butter or margarine and add the icing sugar gradually, beating constantly. Mix in the cocoa, vanilla and coffee and beat until smooth. This quantity fills and ices one 2-layer 20 or 23-cm/8 or 9-in cake.

Marshmallow Frosting

This deluxe frosting is worth the extra beating time.

2 egg whites
225 g/8 oz sugar
$\frac{1}{4}$ teaspoon cream of tartar
1 tablespoon golden syrup
5 tablespoons water
175 g/6 oz chopped marshmallows

In the top of a double boiler, combine the egg whites, sugar, cream of tartar, golden syrup and water. Beat with the electric mixer on low speed for 1 minute. Place over boiling water and beat on high speed until stiff peaks form, about 7 minutes. Remove from the heat and add the marshmallows. Continue beating until the marshmallows have melted. This quantity fills and frosts one 3-layer, 20 or 23-cm/8 or 9-in cake.

Rich Vanilla Icing

Melt-in-your-mouth vanilla icing with chocolate cake makes an excellent flavour contrast

300 ml/½ pint milk
75 g/3 oz flour
350 g/12 oz softened butter or margarine
275 g/10 oz caster sugar
1 teaspoon vanilla essence

In a small saucepan, combine the milk and flour and beat with a wire whisk or electric mixer until smooth. Cook over low heat until thick; cool. In a medium-sized bowl, cream the butter or margarine and sugar until light and fluffy. Beating with an electric mixer on high speed, gradually add the milk-flour mixture. Beat until smooth then stir in the vanilla. This quantity fills and ices one 3-layer, 20 or 23-cm/8 or 9-in cake.

Vanilla Butter Icing

This basic creamy vanilla icing will enhance your favourite chocolate cakes.

100 g/4 oz softened butter or margarine
275 g/10 oz icing sugar
2 teaspoons vanilla essence
2 tablespoons milk
1 to 2 teaspoons more milk, if needed

Blend the butter or margarine and icing sugar in a medium-sized bowl. Stir in the vanilla and milk and beat until smooth, thick and creamy. If necessary, add 1 to 2 teaspoons milk to make the icing spreadable. This quantity ices one 2-layer, 20 or 23-cm/8 or 9-in cake.

Royal Chocolate Sauce

This is the king of chocolate sauces.

100 g/4 oz golden syrup
100 g/4 oz sugar
150 ml/¼ pint water
75 g/3 oz plain chocolate, broken into pieces
1 teaspoon vanilla essence
4 tablespoons evaporated milk, not diluted

In a small saucepan, combine the golden syrup, sugar and water. Cook over medium-low heat to 113 C, 236 F, on a sugar thermometer or to soft-ball stage. Remove from the heat, stir in the chocolate until melted and add the vanilla. Gradually add the evaporated milk, stirring constantly until blended. Cool. Serve over ice cream or cake. Makes 300 ml/½ pint sauce.

Hot Fudge Sauce

375 ml/13 fl oz evaporated milk, not diluted
225 g/8 oz sugar
175 g/6 oz plain chocolate
50 g/2 oz butter or margarine
1 teaspoon vanilla essence
½ teaspoon salt

Bring the milk and sugar to a rolling boil over medium-low heat, stirring constantly; boil and stir for 1 minute longer. Add the chocolate, stir until melted, then beat over heat until smooth. If the sauce has a curdled appearance, beat vigorously with a wire whisk or electric beater until creamy smooth. Remove from heat, blend in the butter or margarine, vanilla and salt. Cool to lukewarm. Serve over ice cream. Makes 900 ml/1½ pints sauce.

Quick Glaze

25 g/1 oz plain chocolate
100 g/4 oz icing sugar
50 g/2 oz butter or margarine
2 tablespoons boiling water

In a small bowl, combine the chocolate and icing sugar. Melt the butter or margarine and chocolate over boiling water and stir until smooth. Makes enough glaze for the top of one 20 or 23-cm/8 or 9-in cake or torte.

Almond Glaze

After you've glazed a favourite cake, you can sprinkle the top with chopped toasted almonds.

175 g/6 oz sugar
3 tablespoons cornflour
300 ml/½ pint water
75 g/3 oz plain chocolate, broken in chunks
25 g/1 oz butter or margarine
1 tablespoon almond-flavoured liqueur

In a medium-sized saucepan, combine the sugar and cornflour. Stir in the water and add the chocolate. Stir constantly over medium heat until thickened. Remove from heat and stir in the butter or margarine and liqueur. Makes enough glaze for the top of one 2-layer, 20 or 23-cm/8 or 9-in cake or torte.

How to glaze a Cake

1 Place the cooled cake upside down on a cake plate. Use your hand or a small brush to remove loose crumbs from the side and top. Spoon the glaze over the top of the cake then spread it evenly with back of spoon or a small palette knife.

2 Spread a small amount of glaze over the edges of cake. A very thin glaze will drip over the side and down to the plate. A thicker glaze may be spread with a palette knife. Many glazes set fast, so work quickly. If the glaze becomes too thick, stir in a few drops of milk or water.

Fudge Sauce

Be sure you melt the chocolate over very low heat.

50 g/2 oz plain chocolate
1 tablespoon butter or margarine
3 tablespoons boiling water
175 g/6 oz sugar
2 tablespoons golden syrup
1 teaspoon vanilla essence

In a small saucepan, over very low heat, melt the chocolate with the butter or margarine, stirring constantly. Add the boiling water, sugar and golden syrup, stirring until the sugar dissolves. Increase the heat to medium-low and simmer for 4 minutes without stirring. Stir in the vanilla and cool to lukewarm. Serve over ice cream or cake. Makes 300 ml/$\frac{1}{2}$ pint sauce.

Fudgy Mint Sauce

100 g/4 oz sugar
150 ml/$\frac{1}{4}$ pint water
2 tablespoons golden syrup
25 g/1 oz butter or margarine
175 g/6 oz plain chocolate drops
1 tablespoon crème de menthe

In a small saucepan, combine the sugar, water, golden syrup and butter or margarine. Bring to a boil over moderate heat, stirring constantly. Simmer for 3 minutes then remove from the heat. Immediately add the chocolate drops. Beat with a wire whisk or electric beater. Stir in the crème de menthe. Serve warm or cool, over ice cream. Makes about 600 ml/1 pint sauce.

Chocolate Chip Sauce

175 g/6 oz plain chocolate, broken into pieces
100 g/4 oz golden syrup
3 tablespoons milk
1 tablespoon butter or margarine
$\frac{1}{4}$ teaspoon vanilla essence

In a small saucepan, combine all the ingredients. Stir constantly over low heat until blended and smooth. Cool. Serve over ice cream. Makes 300 ml/$\frac{1}{2}$ pint sauce.

Mocha Sauce

25 g/1 oz unsweetened cocoa powder
150 m/$\frac{1}{4}$ pint strong coffee
100 g/4 oz honey
3 tablespoons whipping cream

In a small saucepan, combine the cocoa, coffee, honey and cream. Stir constantly over low heat until slightly thickened and smooth. Cool. Serve over ice cream, sponge cake or cream puffs. Makes 300 ml/$\frac{1}{2}$ pint sauce.

Cinnamon-chocolate Sauce

A fine-flavoured, low-calorie topping for angel-food cake or pears.

25 g/1 oz plain chocolate, chopped
2 tablespoons sugar
25 g/1 oz instant nonfat dry milk powder
100 ml/4 fl oz water
$\frac{1}{4}$ teaspoon cinnamon

In a small saucepan, combine the chopped chocolate, sugar, dry milk powder, water and cinnamon. Stir constantly over low heat until smooth. Makes 150 ml/$\frac{1}{4}$ pint sauce, about 35 calories per tablespoon.

Custard Cream Filling

The final touch of perfection for Éclairs (page 108) or Cream Puffs (page 109).

50 g/2 oz sugar
1 tablespoon flour
1 tablespoon cornflour
$\frac{1}{4}$ teaspoon salt
350 ml/12 fl oz milk
1 egg yolk, slightly beaten
1 teaspoon vanilla essence
150 ml/$\frac{1}{4}$ pint whipping cream

In a medium-sized saucepan, combine the sugar, flour, cornflour and salt. Gradually stir in the milk. Stir constantly over medium heat until the mixture boils and thickens. Remove from the heat. Stir a small amount of hot milk mixture into the egg yolk. Add the egg yolk mixture to the remaining hot milk mixture in the saucepan. Stir over low heat for another 2 minutes. Stir in the vanilla. Cover the surface with cling film then cool. Whip the cream and fold it into the cool custard. Makes enough to fill 10 éclairs or 9 cream puffs.

Cream Filling

Creamy texture, mild chocolate flavour and a light chocolate colour.

50 g/2 oz sugar
25 g/1 oz flour
300 ml/$\frac{1}{2}$ pint milk
1 egg, lightly beaten
25 g/1 oz plain chocolate, melted
1 teaspoon vanilla essence

In a small saucepan, combine the sugar and flour. Stir in the milk then stir constantly over low heat until smooth and thickened. Remove from heat and stir a small amount of hot mixture into the egg. Add the egg mixture to the remaining hot mixture in the saucepan. Mix in the chocolate. Stir constantly over very low heat for 1 minute longer then remove from heat. Stir in the vanilla, cover and chill. Use as a filling for a sandwich cake or Swiss roll. Makes about 450 ml/$\frac{3}{4}$ pint filling.

Minty Marshmallow Filling

3 tablespoons crème de menthe
$\frac{1}{2}$ quantity Marshmallow Frosting (page 36)
300 ml/$\frac{1}{2}$ pint whipping cream

In a medium-sized bowl, stir the crème de menthe into the Marshmallow Frosting. Whip the cream in a small bowl and fold the whipped cream and food colouring into the marshmallow mixture. Use as a filling for chocolate cups, Swiss roll, chocolate cakes or baked meringues. Makes 1.15 litres/2 pints filling.

Fluffy Filling

175 g/6 oz plain chocolate, broken into pieces
100 g/4 oz softened butter or margarine
75 g/3 oz icing sugar
2 eggs, separated
1 teaspoon vanilla essence

Melt the chocolate pieces and set aside. In a medium-sized bowl, cream the butter or margarine and icing sugar until light and fluffy. Add the egg yolks one at a time, beating after each addition. Gradually beat in the melted chocolate and vanilla. In a small bowl, beat the egg whites until stiff but not dry and fold them into the chocolate mixture. Use as a filling for cakes, cream puffs or éclairs. Makes about 600 ml/1 pint filling.

Buns, Bars and Biscuits

This chapter is loaded with all kinds of goodies just brimming with chocolate. Especially irresistible is our collection of brownies and other bar-type biscuits. If you like your biscuits plain and simple, you'll enjoy making Crinkles and Soured Cream Cookies, while those of us who like the challenge of specially shaped treats will be tempted by Acorn Biscuits and Pretzel Cookies.

You'll notice that chocolate appears in many forms in these biscuits: be sure to use the kind of chocolate indicated in the recipe. If a recipe calls for either plain or milk chocolate drops, with no mention of melting the chocolate, you will be stirring the little pieces into the biscuit mixture. They soften in the baking process but do not melt: the tiny drops of chocolate retain their original size and shape. On the other hand, if the recipe calls for melted chocolate, you can follow the directions for melting chocolate given on pages 11 and 12, then stir the melted chocolate into the mixture. When baked, the whole biscuit will be a chocolate colour.

Although you can re-use the same baking tray for cooking the drop-type and shaped biscuits, you can hurry the baking process by using two or more trays. While one batch of biscuits is baking, you can be getting another ready for the oven. Be sure to let the tins cool before placing the uncooked dough on them. Also, biscuit dough spreads in the baking, so don't place the biscuits too close together on the baking tray.

Fudge Brownies

75 g/3 oz butter or margarine
75 g/3 oz plain chocolate
2 eggs
175 g/6 oz sugar
$\frac{1}{4}$ teaspoon salt
$\frac{1}{2}$ teaspoon vanilla essence
75 g/3 oz plain flour
50 g/2 oz chopped nuts

In a small saucepan, melt the butter or margarine and chocolate over low heat; set aside to cool. Set the oven at 180 C, 350 F, gas 4. In a medium-sized bowl, beat the eggs until light and foamy. Beat in the sugar and add the salt and vanilla. Stir in the cooled chocolate mixture, then stir in the flour. Fold in the nuts. Bake in an ungreased 20-cm/8-in square tin for about 20 minutes or until the edges begin to leave the sides of the tin. Cool in the tin before cutting. **Makes 16 brownies.**

Hazel's Brownies

These are perfect for picnics or lunch boxes.

175 g/6 oz butter or margarine, melted
175 g/6 oz sugar
1 teaspoon vanilla essence
$\frac{1}{4}$ teaspoon salt
3 eggs
50 g/2 oz unsweetened cocoa powder
$\frac{1}{2}$ teaspoon baking powder
175 g/6 oz plain flour
50 g/2 oz chopped nuts

Butter a 20-cm/8-in square baking tin and set it aside. Set the oven at 180 C, 350 F, gas 4. In a large bowl, combine the melted butter or margarine and sugar. Beat until blended. Add the vanilla, salt and eggs and beat well. Add the cocoa, baking powder and flour, mixing until smooth. Stir in the nuts. Pour into the prepared tin and bake for 25 to 30 minutes. Cool in the tin before cutting. **Makes 16 to 20 brownies.**

Cream Cheese Brownies

The little extra preparation time is well worth the trouble.

25 g/1 oz butter
100 g/4 oz cooking chocolate
25 g/1 oz softened butter or margarine
75 g/3 oz cream cheese, at room temperature
150 g/6 oz sugar
3 eggs
1 tablespoon flour
1 teaspoon vanilla essence
100 g/4 oz sugar
50 g/2 oz flour
$\frac{1}{2}$ teaspoon baking powder
$\frac{1}{2}$ teaspoon salt
50 g/2 oz chopped walnuts
1 teaspoon vanilla essence
$\frac{1}{4}$ teaspoon almond essence

In the top of a double boiler over hot water, melt the butter and chocolate. Remove from the hot water and set aside to cool. Grease a 23-cm/9-in square baking tin; set aside. Set the oven at 180 C, 350 F, gas 4. In a medium-sized bowl, cream the softened butter or margarine with the cream cheese until fluffy. Beat in 50 g/2 oz of the sugar, 1 egg, the tablespoon of flour and the vanilla; set aside. In a large bowl, beat the remaining eggs until foamy. Add the rest of the sugar; continue beating until blended. Stir in the 50 g/2 oz flour, baking powder and salt, then the melted chocolate mixture, walnuts, vanilla and almond essences. Spread half of the chocolate mixture evenly in the prepared tin. Spread the cream cheese mixture on top. Drop spoonfuls of the remaining chocolate mixture on top of the cream cheese mixture. Swirl the top slightly with a fork. Bake for 40 to 50 minutes or until the edges begin to leave sides of tin. Cool in the tin before cutting. **Makes 16 brownies.**

Fudge Brownies

Peanut Butter Brownies

Easy-to-make peanut squares with a strong chocolate flavour.

75 g/3 oz plain chocolate
50 g/2 oz butter or margarine
25 g/1 oz peanut butter
175 g/6 oz demerara or soft brown sugar
2 eggs
1 teaspoon vanilla essence
100 g/4 oz flour
50 g/2 oz chopped peanuts

Melt the chocolate and set it aside to cool. Grease an 18-cm/7-in square tin; set aside. Set the oven at 160 C, 325 F, gas 3. In a medium-sized bowl, cream the butter or margarine, peanut butter and brown sugar. Beat in the eggs and vanilla. Mix in the melted chocolate, then the flour and stir in the peanuts. Pour into the prepared tin. Bake for 30 to 35 minutes or until the edges begin to leave the sides of the tin. Cool in the tin before cutting. **Makes 16 brownies.**

Double-decker Biscuits

100 g/4 oz softened butter or margarine
150 g/5 oz sugar
1 egg
1 teaspoon vanilla essence
225 g/8 oz flour
$\frac{1}{4}$ teaspoon salt
1 teaspoon baking powder
75 g/3 oz milk chocolate
$\frac{1}{2}$ quantity Marshmallow Frosting (page 36)

Grease a 20-cm/8-in square baking tin. Set the oven at 180 C, 350 F, gas 4. In a large bowl, cream the butter or margarine and sugar until light and fluffy. Beat in the egg and vanilla. Add the flour, salt and baking powder and beat again until well mixed. Press half of the dough into the bottom of the prepared tin. Break the milk chocolate into small pieces and arrange them over the dough. Spread with the marshmallow frosting. Drop the remaining dough over the filling in small patches. If possible, gently spread over the Marshmallow Frosting. Bake for 25 to 30 minutes or until golden brown. Cool in the tin before cutting. **Makes 16 squares.**

Peanut Butter Dreams

An exquisite blend of chocolate and coconut on a peanut butter crust.

75 g/3 oz peanut butter
50 g/2 oz softened butter or margarine
100 g/4 oz demerara or soft brown sugar
100 g/4 oz plain flour
Coconut-chocolate Topping (see below)
COCONUT-CHOCOLATE TOPPING
2 eggs
100 g/4 oz demerara or soft brown sugar
1 teaspoon vanilla essence
15 g/$\frac{1}{2}$ oz flour
$\frac{1}{2}$ teaspoon baking powder
$\frac{1}{2}$ teaspoon salt
50 g/2 oz desiccated coconut
175 g/6 oz plain chocolate drops

Set the oven at 180 C, 350 F, gas 4. In a medium-sized bowl, blend the peanut butter, butter or margarine and sugar. Stir in the flour. Turn into an ungreased 33 × 23 cm/13 × 9 in baking tin. Flatten the dough with your hand to cover the bottom of the tin. Bake for 10 minutes. While it is baking, prepare the Coconut-chocolate Topping. Spread the topping on the baked crust. Return to the oven and bake for 25 minutes or until golden brown. Cool in the tin before cutting into 2.5 × 7.5 cm/1 × 3 in bars. **Makes about 39 bars.**

Coconut-chocolate Topping

In a medium-sized bowl, beat the eggs well. Add the brown sugar and vanilla and beat until blended. Mix in the flour, baking powder and salt. Stir in the coconut and chocolate drops.

Butterscotch Bars

Cornflakes add a crunchy surprise to these satisfying bars.

225 g/8 oz plain flour
100 g/4 oz demerara or soft brown sugar
175 g/6 oz butter or margarine
225 g/8 oz granulated sugar
350 g/12 oz golden syrup
175 g/6 oz butterscotch, broken into pieces
350 g/12 oz peanut butter
75 g/3 oz cornflakes
Creamy Chocolate Icing (see below)
CREAMY CHOCOLATE ICING
75 g/3 oz plain chocolate, broken into pieces
25 g/1 oz butter or margarine
1 tablespoon milk
25 g/1 oz icing sugar
$\frac{1}{2}$ teaspoon vanilla essence

Set the oven at 180 C, 350 F, gas 4. In a small bowl, blend the flour, brown sugar and butter or margarine with an electric mixer on low speed; the mixture will be crumbly. Press into the bottom of an ungreased 33 × 23-cm/13 × 9-in baking tin and bake for 15 to 20 minutes. Meanwhile, bring the granulated sugar and golden syrup to a boil in a large saucepan over medium heat, stirring occasionally. Remove from the heat, add the butterscotch pieces and peanut butter and stir until melted. Stir in the cornflakes. Spread over the baked crust and leave to cool. Prepare the Creamy Chocolate Icing. Ice the cooled cake before cutting into 2.5 × 7.5-cm/1 × 3-in bars. **Makes 39 bars.**

Creamy Chocolate Icing

Combine the chocolate pieces, butter or margarine and milk in a small saucepan. Place over low heat until the chocolate and butter or margarine are melted. Remove from the heat, add icing sugar and vanilla and mix well.

Rocky Road Bars

Scrumptious melted marshmallows and chocolate topping over nutty chocolate bars.

75 g/3 oz butter or margarine
25 g/1 oz plain chocolate
225 g/8 oz sugar
2 eggs, beaten
100 g/4 oz flour
$\frac{1}{2}$ teaspoon salt
$\frac{1}{2}$ teaspoon baking powder
1 teaspoon vanilla essence
50 g/2 oz chopped walnuts
20 marshmallows, halved
Chocolate Topping (see below)
CHOCOLATE TOPPING
50 g/2 oz plain chocolate
50 g/2 oz butter or margarine
225 g/8 oz icing sugar
4 tablespoons milk
1 teaspoon vanilla essence

Grease a 28 × 18-cm/11 × 7-in baking tin and set it aside. Set the oven at 180 C, 350 F, gas 4. Melt the butter or margarine and chocolate over low heat. Remove from the heat and beat in the sugar, then the eggs. Combine the flour, salt and baking powder and stir into the chocolate mixture. Add the vanilla and walnuts. Pour into the prepared tin and bake for 35 minutes. Remove from the oven and immediately top with marshmallows. Return to the oven for 3 minutes or until the marshmallows are soft. Set aside while preparing the Chocolate Topping. Pour the topping over the warm marshmallows then leave to cool in the tin before cutting. **Makes 33 bars.**

Chocolate Topping

Combine the chocolate and butter or margarine in a small saucepan and place over a low heat until just melted. Combine the icing sugar, milk and vanilla in a bowl, add the chocolate mixture and beat until smooth.

Crunchy Almond Bars

225 g/8 oz soft margarine
225 g/8 oz sugar
1 egg
$\frac{1}{4}$ teaspoon almond essence
250 g/9 oz plain flour
$\frac{1}{2}$ teaspoon baking powder
$1\frac{1}{2}$ teaspoons salt
50 g/2 oz toasted slivered almonds
100 g/4 oz glacé cherries, halved
50 g/2 oz desiccated coconut
175 g/6 oz plain chocolate drops
Simply Sweet Glaze (see below)
sliced glacé cherries for decoration
SIMPLY SWEET GLAZE
1 tablespoon butter
1 tablespoon milk
100 g/4 oz sifted icing sugar

Grease two 40 × 33-cm/16 × 11-in baking tin and set it aside. Set the oven at 190 C, 375 F, gas 5. In a large bowl, cream the soft margarine and sugar until light and creamy. Beat in the egg and almond essence. Add the flour, baking powder and salt and mix well. Stir in the almonds, glacé cherries, coconut and chocolate drops. Spread in the prepared tin and bake for 20 minutes. Cool slightly. Meanwhile, prepare the Simply Sweet Glaze and drizzle it over the warm cake. Cut into 2.5 × 5-cm/1 × 2-in bars. Decorate each bar with a cherry slice. **Makes about 70 bars.**

Simply Sweet Glaze

In a small saucepan, melt the butter or margarine with the milk over low heat. Remove from the heat and stir in the icing sugar until creamy.

Cherry Chocolate Bars

Illustrated on page 51

225 g/8 oz digestive biscuits, finely crushed
175 g/6 oz plain chocolate drops
1 (397-g/14-oz) can sweetened condensed milk
40 g/1$\frac{1}{2}$ oz desiccated coconut
50 g/2 oz chopped nuts
100 g/4 oz chopped glacé cherries

Grease a 18-cm/7-in square baking tin and set it aside. Set the oven at 180 C, 350 F, gas 4. In a medium-sized bowl, combine the digestive biscuit crumbs, the chocolate drops, milk, coconut, nuts and cherries. Spoon into the prepared tin and bake for 25 to 30 minutes. Cool in the tin before cutting. **Makes 16 squares.**

Pinwheels

100 g/4 oz softened butter or margarine
175 g/6 oz sugar
1 egg
1 teaspoon vanilla essence
175 g/6 oz plain flour
$\frac{1}{4}$ teaspoon salt
2 tablespoons unsweetened cocoa powder

In a large bowl, cream the butter or margarine, sugar and egg until light and fluffy. Stir in the vanilla. Add the flour and salt and mix until blended. Divide the dough in half. Add the cocoa to one half. Cover and refrigerate both halves for several hours or until firm. On floured waxed paper, roll each half of dough to a 40 × 15-cm/16 × 6-in rectangle. Invert the white dough onto the chocolate dough; peel the waxed paper off the white dough. Tightly roll up both doughs together, peeling the waxed paper off the chocolate dough as you roll. Cover the rolls and refrigerate for several hours or overnight. Set the oven at 200 C, 400 F, gas 6. Slice the roll 5 m/$\frac{1}{4}$ in thick. If the dough becomes soft while slicing, refrigerate briefly. Bake on ungreased baking trays for 5 to 7 minutes or until lightly browned. Cool on a wire rack. **Makes 60 to 65 pinwheels.**

How to make Pinwheels

1 To form a two-toned pinwheel biscuit, you'll need equal amounts of white or plain and chocolate dough. Refrigerate both doughs several hours for easier handling. Then, on a small piece of waxed paper, roll out each dough to a 40 × 15-cm/16 × 6-in rectangle.

2 Working as quickly as possible, invert the plain dough rectangle over the chocolate rectangle. Carefully peel off the waxed paper from the plain dough.

3 With both hands, tightly roll up the doughs together. Peel the waxed paper off the chocolate dough as you roll. Cover and chill for several hours before slicing.

4 With a sharp knife, slice the chilled dough crosswise about 5 mm/$\frac{1}{4}$ in thick. If the dough begins to soften, refrigerate it and when the dough is firm again, continue slicing.

Spicy Apple and Peanut Bars

75 g/3 oz soft margarine
175 g/6 oz sugar
2 eggs
75 g/3 oz plain flour
$\frac{3}{4}$ teaspoon baking powder
$\frac{1}{2}$ teaspoon bicarbonate of soda
$\frac{1}{2}$ teaspoon salt
1 tablespoon unsweetened cocoa powder
1 teaspoon cinnamon
$\frac{1}{2}$ teaspoon nutmeg
$\frac{1}{4}$ teaspoon ground cloves
100 g/4 oz uncooked rolled oats
175 g/6 oz diced peeled apple
50 g/2 oz chopped peanuts
icing sugar

Lightly grease a 25-cm/9-in square baking tin and set it aside. Set the oven at 190 C, 375 F, gas 5. In a large bowl, cream the margarine and sugar until light and fluffy. Add the eggs one at a time, beating until very light and fluffy. Combine the flour, baking powder, bicarbonate of soda, salt, cocoa, cinnamon, nutmeg and cloves. With an electric mixer on low speed, beat the flour mixture into the egg mixture until just combined. Stir in the oats, apple and peanuts and turn the mixture into the prepared tin. Bake for 25 minutes or until the edges begin to leave the sides of the tin. Cool completely before cutting. Sprinkle with the icing sugar. **Makes 18 bars.**

Butter Walnut Turtles

175 g/6 oz flour
225 g/8 oz demerara or soft brown sugar
75 g/3 oz softened butter
50 g/2 oz chopped walnuts
100 g/4 oz butter or margarine
175 g/6 oz milk chocolate drops.

Set the oven at 180 C, 350 F, gas 4. Place the flour and 175 g/6 oz of the sugar in a medium-sized bowl. With pastry blender or fork, cut in the softened butter until crumbly and well-mixed. Press firmly into the bottom of an ungreased 23-cm/9-in square baking tin. Sprinkle the walnuts over the top. In a small saucepan, bring the 100 g/4 oz butter or margarine and the remaining sugar to a boil. Simmer for 1 minute, stirring constantly. Remove from the heat and gently pour over the walnuts, covering all the pastry if possible. Bake for 15 to 20 minutes or until the caramel is bubbly over its entire surface. Remove from the oven and immediately sprinkle it with chocolate drops. Let stand to slightly melt the chocolate, then gently swirl a palette knife through the caramel and chocolate to create a marbled effect. Cool in the tin before cutting. **Makes 25 bars.**

Double-chocolate Biscuits

100 g/4 oz softened butter or margarine
225 g/8 oz sugar
1 egg
300 ml/$\frac{1}{2}$ pint soured cream
1 teaspoon vanilla essence
225 g/8 oz plain flour
50 g/2 oz unsweetened cocoa powder
$\frac{1}{2}$ teaspoon bicarbonate of soda
$\frac{1}{2}$ teaspoon salt
75 g/3 oz plain chocolate drops

Grease two baking trays; set aside. Set the oven at 190 C, 375 F, gas 5. In a large bowl, beat the butter or margarine and sugar until fluffy. Beat in the egg, then the soured cream and vanilla. Combine the flour, cocoa, bicarbonate of soda and salt. Gradually beat into the creamed mixture and stir in the chocolate drops. Drop from a teaspoon onto prepared baking trays. Bake for 8 to 10 minutes. Cool slightly before transferring to wire racks. **Makes about 60 biscuits.**

Orange Oatmeal Drops

100 g / 4 oz margarine
225 g / 8 oz demerara or soft brown sugar
1 egg
1 teaspoon grated orange rind
1 tablespoon orange juice
50 g / 2 oz plain flour
$\frac{1}{4}$ teaspoon bicarbonate of soda
150 g / 5 oz uncooked quick-cooking rolled oats
175 g / 6 oz plain chocolate drops
50 g / 2 oz chopped walnuts

Grease two baking trays; set aside. Set the oven at 190 C, 375 F, gas 5. In a large bowl, cream the margarine and brown sugar. Beat in the egg, orange rind and juice. Add the flour and bicarbonate of soda. Beat until smooth. Stir in the oats, chocolate drops and walnuts. Drop from a teaspoon onto prepared baking trays. Bake for 10 to 12 minutes or until light brown. **Makes 36 to 48 biscuits.**

Jumbo Chippers

100 g / 4 oz butter or margarine
40 g / 2$\frac{1}{2}$ oz granulated sugar
75 g / 3 oz soft brown sugar
$\frac{1}{2}$ teaspoon vanilla essence
$\frac{1}{4}$ teaspoon water
1 egg
125 g / 4$\frac{1}{2}$ oz flour
$\frac{1}{2}$ teaspoon bicarbonate of soda
$\frac{1}{2}$ teaspoon salt
175 g / 6 oz plain chocolate drops
50 g / 2 oz chopped peanuts

Grease 2 baking trays and set aside. Set the oven at 180 C, 350 F, gas 4. In a large bowl, cream the butter or margarine, granulated and brown sugars, vanilla and water. Beat in the egg. Add the flour, bicarbonate of soda and salt. Mix well. Stir in the chocolate drops and peanuts. This will make about 450 g / 1 lb dough. Spread one-tenth of the dough into a 10-cm / 4-in circle on the prepared baking tray. Repeat until all the dough is used up and 10 are formed. Bake 10 to 12 minutes. Place on a wire rack to cool. **Makes 10 chippers.**

Jumbo Chipper Sandwiches

50 g / 2 oz butter or margarine
50 g / 2 oz peanut butter
225 g / 8 oz icing sugar
$\frac{1}{2}$ teaspoon vanilla essence
3 tablespoons milk
10 Jumbo Chippers, cooled (see opposite)

In a medium-sized bowl, cream the butter or margarine and peanut butter. Add the icing sugar, vanilla and milk. Beat until smooth. Spread generously on 5 Jumbo Chippers and top with the remaining Jumbo Chippers. **Makes 5 sandwiches.**

Banana Granola Biscuits

Mashed bananas and treacle make a tasty, moist biscuit base.

75 g / 3 oz margarine
100 g / 4 oz demerara or soft brown sugar
75 g / 3 oz treacle
1 egg
4 ripe bananas, mashed
40 g / 1$\frac{1}{2}$ oz powdered milk
150 g / 5 oz plain flour
1 teaspoon baking powder
$\frac{1}{2}$ teaspoon bicarbonate of soda
$\frac{1}{4}$ teaspoon salt
$\frac{1}{8}$ teaspoon ground ginger
225 g / 8 oz granola cereal
175 g / 6 oz plain chocolate drops

Grease two baking trays and set them aside. Set the oven at 180 C, 350 F, gas 4. In a large bowl, cream the margarine and brown sugar. Beat in the treacle and egg. Stir in the mashed bananas and dry milk. Combine the flour, baking powder, bicarbonate of soda, salt, and ginger and blend into the creamed mixture. Stir in the granola and chocolate drops. Drop from a teaspoon onto prepared baking trays and bake for 10 to 12 minutes. Cool on wire racks. **Makes about 48 biscuits.**

Acorn Biscuits

225 g/8 oz butter, softened
175 g/6 oz demerara or soft brown sugar
1 teaspoon vanilla essence
300 g/11 oz flour
$\frac{1}{2}$ teaspoon baking powder
175 g/6 oz plain chocolate, broken into pieces
50 g/2 oz finely chopped pecans or walnuts

Set the oven at 180 C, 350 F, gas 4. In a medium-sized bowl, cream the butter, brown sugar and vanilla. Stir in the flour and baking powder. Using a rounded teaspoonful of dough for each biscuit, shape into balls. Pinch the dough to a rounded point at one end to resemble an acorn. Place each on a baking tray either upright, rounded point up, or lying on one side. Bake for about 15 minutes or until golden brown. Cool. Melt the chocolate over hot but not boiling water. Dip the large end of each cooled acorn biscuit first in the chocolate, then in the chopped nuts. **Makes 48 acorns.**

Spritz Biscuits

3 tablespoons boiling water
6 tablespoons unsweetened cocoa powder
225 g/8 oz softened butter
1 teaspoon vanilla essence
100 g/4 oz sugar
1 egg yolk
225 g/8 oz plain flour
$\frac{1}{2}$ teaspoon baking powder
$\frac{1}{4}$ teaspoon salt

In a small bowl, thoroughly blend the boiling water and cocoa and set aside to cool. Set the oven at 180 C, 350 F, gas 4. In a large bowl, cream the butter and vanilla and add the sugar gradually, beating until light and fluffy. Add the egg yolk and beat thoroughly. Stir in the cocoa mixture. Combine the flour, baking powder and salt. Add to the creamed mixture a quarter at a time, mixing until blended after each addition. Put the dough through a biscuit former or shape with biscuit cutters and put onto an ungreased baking tray. Bake for 12 minutes; cool on wire racks. **Makes 60 to 70 biscuits.**

Pecan Rounds

50 g/2 oz plain chocolate
225 g/8 oz softened butter or margarine
225 g/8 oz sugar
1 teaspoon vanilla essence
225 g/8 oz flour
$\frac{1}{4}$ teaspoon baking powder
$\frac{1}{4}$ teaspoon bicarbonate of soda
finely chopped pecans or walnuts
$\frac{1}{2}$ teaspoon cinnamon
pecan or walnut halves for decoration

Melt the chocolate and set it aside to cool. Set the oven at 180 C, 350 F, gas 4. In a large bowl, cream the butter or margarine and 175 g/6 oz of the sugar. Stir in the vanilla and melted chocolate. Combine the flour, baking powder and bicarbonate of soda. Stir into the chocolate mixture and add the chopped pecans or walnuts. Form into 2.5-cm/1-in balls. If the dough is too soft to handle, refrigerate for a few minutes. Mix together the remaining sugar and the cinnamon and roll the balls in this mixture. Press a pecan or walnut half on top of each. Bake on ungreased baking trays for 12 to 15 minutes or until firm. **Makes about 55 biscuits.**

From the top Pecan Rounds (above), Cherry Chocolate Bars (page 46), Acorn Biscuits and Spritz Biscuits (above)

Soured Cream Cookies

50 g/2 oz plain chocolate
175 g/6 oz softened butter or margarine
275 g/10 oz sugar
1 teaspoon vanilla essence
1 egg
6 tablespoons soured cream
200 g/7 oz plain flour
½ teaspoon baking powder
½ teaspoon bicarbonate of soda
½ teaspoon salt
50 g/2 oz chopped nuts

Grease two baking trays and set them aside. Melt the chocolate; set aside also. Set the oven at 220 C, 425 F, gas 7. In a large bowl, cream the butter or margarine then gradually beat in the sugar, creaming well. Add the vanilla and egg, beating until fluffy. Stir in the melted chocolate, then the soured cream. Add the flour, baking powder, bicarbonate of soda and salt. Stir until well mixed then stir in the nuts. Drop heaped teaspoonfuls onto prepared baking trays and bake for about 8 minutes. Cool slightly before placing on wire racks. **Makes about 48 cookies.**

Banana Oatmeal Drops

175 g/6 oz softened butter or margarine
225 g/8 oz demerara or soft brown sugar
1 egg
2 large ripe bananas, mashed
175 g/6 oz flour
½ teaspoon salt
½ teaspoon bicarbonate of soda
½ teaspoon nutmeg
150 g/5 oz uncooked quick-cooking rolled oats
175 g/6 oz plain chocolate drops

Set the oven at 200 C, 400 F, gas 6. In a large bowl, beat the butter or margarine, sugar and egg until light and fluffy. Beat in the bananas. Combine the flour, salt, bicarbonate of soda and nutmeg, and gradually beat it into the egg mixture. Stir in the oats and chocolate drops. Drop from a teaspoon onto ungreased baking trays 5 cm/2 in apart. Bake for 12 to 15 minutes or until golden. Cool on wire racks. **Makes 75 to 80 drops.**

Crinkles

The tops of these biscuits resemble tortoiseshell.

50 g/2 oz plain chocolate
100 g/4 oz soft margarine
350 g/12 oz sugar
2 teaspoons vanilla essence
2 eggs
225 g/8 oz plain flour
2 teaspoons baking powder
½ teaspoon salt
5 tablespoons milk
50 g/2 oz chopped walnuts
sifted icing sugar

Melt the chocolate and set it aside to cool. In a large bowl, thoroughly cream the soft margarine, sugar and vanilla. Beat in the eggs, then the melted chocolate. Combine the flour, baking powder and salt. Add alternately with the milk to the chocolate mixture and beat until blended. Stir in the walnuts. Chill for several hours. When ready to bake, set the oven at 180 C, 350 F, gas 4. Grease 2 baking trays. Form the dough into 2.5-cm/1-in balls and roll them in sifted icing sugar. Place on the prepared baking trays 5 to 7.5 cm/2 to 3 in apart. Bake for 15 minutes. Cool slightly before placing on wire racks. **Makes about 48 biscuits.**

Chocolate Macaroons

These have a chewy consistency and superb flavour.

175 g/6 oz plain chocolate, broken into pieces
3 egg whites
¼ teaspoon salt
225 g/8 oz sugar
50 g/2 oz ground blanched almonds
½ teaspoon vanilla essence

Melt the chocolate pieces and leave to cool. Grease the baking trays; set aside also. Set the oven at 180 C, 350 F, gas 4. Beat the egg whites and salt until stiff but not dry and gradually beat in the sugar until the mixture is thick and glossy. Fold in the almonds, vanilla and melted chocolate. Drop from a teaspoon onto baking trays and bake for 15 minutes. Cool on wire racks. **Makes 36 to 40 macaroons.**

Marshmallow Sandwich Biscuits

225 g/8 oz flour
1 teaspoon bicarbonate of soda
¼ teaspoon salt
25 g/1 oz unsweetened cocoa powder
225 g/8 oz granulated sugar
1 egg
4 tablespoons cooking oil
1 teaspoon vanilla essence
175 ml/6 fl oz milk
100 g/4 oz butter or margarine
100 g/4 oz icing sugar

Grease a baking tray and set it aside. Set the oven at 180 C, 350 F, gas 4. In a large bowl, combine the flour, bicarbonate of soda, salt, cocoa and granulated sugar. Make a well in centre of the mixture, add the egg, oil, vanilla and milk and beat until smooth. Drop by rounded tablespoonfuls onto prepared baking trays about 7.5 cm/3 in apart. Bake for 10 to 12 minutes and cool on a wire rack. In a small bowl, combine the butter or margarine and icing sugar and beat until smooth. Spread the cream filling on half the cooled biscuits and top with the remainder. **Makes about 14 biscuits.**

Kissing Cookies

100 g/4 oz softened butter or margarine
175 g/6 oz creamy peanut butter
175 g/6 oz granulated sugar
60 g/2½ oz demerara or soft brown sugar
1 egg
2 tablespoons milk
1 teaspoon vanilla essence
175 g/6 oz flour
1 teaspoon bicarbonate of soda
½ teaspoon salt
250 g/9 oz milk chocolate buttons

Set the oven at 190 C, 375 F, gas 4. In a large bowl, cream the butter or margarine and peanut butter. Gradually beat in 50 g/2 oz granulated sugar and the demerara sugar until light and fluffy. Add the egg, milk and vanilla and mix well. Combine the flour, bicarbonate of soda and salt. Gradually blend into the creamed mixture. Shape the dough into 2.5-cm/1-in balls. Roll in the remaining granulated sugar. Place on ungreased baking trays. Bake for 10 to 12 minutes or until cracked and light brown. Remove from the oven and immediately press a chocolate button firmly into the centre of each cookie. Carefully remove from the baking tray. Cool on wire racks until the chocolate is set, about 2 hours. **Makes 48 to 50 cookies.**

Pretzel Cookies

Almond cookies in a new, surprise shape

225 g/8 oz butter or margarine, softened
225 g/8 oz sugar
3 egg yolks
100 g/4 oz ground unblanched almonds
¼ teaspoon almond essence
1 teaspoon grated lemon rind
250 g/9 oz plain flour
Cookie Glaze (see below)
COOKIE GLAZE
350 g/12 oz plain chocolate, broken into pieces
75 g/3 oz golden syrup
175 ml/6 fl oz milk
15 g/½ oz butter or margarine

In a large bowl, beat the butter or margarine and sugar until fluffy. Add the egg yolks one at a time, beating well after each addition. Add the almonds, almond essence and lemon rind. Gradually add the flour, mixing until the dough is smooth. Cover and refrigerate for 2 hours. Grease 2 baking sheets and set them aside. Set the oven at 180 C, 350 F, gas 4. Form the dough into balls using about 1 tablespoon dough for each. On a lightly floured board, using the palms of the hands, form each ball into a 25-cm/10-in-long roll. Twist into a pretzel shape and place on the prepared baking trays about 5 cm/2 in apart. Bake for 10 to 12 minutes or until light brown. Cool on a wire rack on top of waxed paper or foil. Prepare Cookie Glaze and carefully spoon it over the warm cookies. Cool. **Makes about 40 cookies.**

Cookie Glaze

While the cookies are baking, combine the chocolate pieces, golden syrup, milk and butter or margarine in a small saucepan. Stir constantly over low heat until the chocolate melts.

Confectionery

Making confectionery can be great fun, and it can be a family or party project, what with buttering and preparing moulds and ingredients, cooking, beating and forming or cutting assigned to the various participants. Usually they join in eagerly because the anticipation of the fruits of their labour overcomes all thoughts of confectionery making as work.

The economics of making your own confectionery has to be a distinct plus. The homemade kind is far less expensive than the commercial product and also, in most cases, is not a tedious and time-consuming process. A spur-of-the-moment craving for fudge can often and quite easily be satisfied by a short confectionery-making session.

When making confectionery, the most critical phase is judging when to stop the cooking process. This is difficult to determine by cooking time, because no two stoves cook at exactly the same heat intensity on the identical heat settings. That's why it's best to rely on thermometer readings, the cold water test overleaf, or on both methods.

To test the accuracy of your sugar thermometer, place it in a pan of warm water. Gradually bring the water to a boil and boil for 10 minutes. The thermometer should read 100 C, 212 F. If it doesn't, add or subtract the number of degrees necessary for accuracy in cooking.

The Art of Dipping Chocolate

Why would you want to spend your time dipping chocolates when you can buy such beautifully made confections? It's fun, that's true, but for a beginner it can be extremely frustrating.

However, you're determined to give it a try anyway, and that's the first step to dipping chocolates successfully. You have to *want to learn how.*

If you've ever bitten into an expensive but stale chocolate, you will appreciate your own chocolates. You will know the quality, flavour and freshness of the ingredients. Also, homemade chocolates are less expensive than comparable ones you can buy.

Although dipping chocolate is a practical and rewarding activity, it is a slow process and should not be hurried. Allow several hours for your project.

Like many hobbies, this may be difficult at first, but it is rewarding when you produce something beautiful. Dipping chocolates is a hobby that a family or a group can share. Think of the impressive array of confectionery you can make for Christmas!

There's no magic formula for beautiful, glossy chocolate-coated confections that can compare with the elegant commercial beauties. But keep trying—you'll be surprised!

Butter-nut Crunch (page 68)

Cold-water Test

Stage	Temperature	When a small amount of syrup is dropped into a cup of cold water:
Soft ball	234° to 240°F 112° to 116°C	Syrup doesn't disintegrate but forms a recognisable soft ball that flattens on your finger when removed from water.
Firm ball	244° to 248°F 118° to 120°C	Syrup holds ball shape when removed from water and flattens easily with slight finger pressure.
Hard ball	250° to 266°F	Syrup holds ball shape when removed from water, shows slight resistence to finger pressure and is pliable.
Soft crack	270° to 290°F 132° to 143°C	Syrup forms firm but not brittle threads.
Hard crack	300° to 310°F 149° to 154°C	Syrup forms hard and brittle threads.

Dipping Chocolates

Choosing Your Chocolate

Several kinds of chocolate can be used for dipping. The kind you choose should depend on taste, colour and how easy it is to work with.

Dipping Chocolate Specially prepared for dipping, it is much the easiest to use for this job. This chocolate is very occasionally available from high-class confectioners, especially ones that make their own chocolates.

Milk chocolate and plain chocolate pieces We found equal parts of milk chocolate and plain chocolate, in pieces, are the most practical combination for dipping. This blend provides a flavour that is a cross between dark and milk chocolate and has a very appealing colour.

On the Way to Success

● Cut and shape sweet centres before preparing chocolate. Flat, thin centres are harder to dip than rounded or cubed ones.
● Don't make the centres too large. Remember, chocolate coating adds to the size of the sweets.
● The centres should be at room temperature when dipping.
● Make sure all your equipment and utensils are clean and dry.
● Less than 350 g/12 oz melted chocolate is difficult to dip into. More than 1 kg/2 lb is hard to handle. Work with an amount in between.
● The ideal temperature for dipping varies with the kind of chocolate. Unless you are experienced in chocolate dipping, use the exact combination of chocolate and temperature we suggest. The temperature of the room as well as the temperature of the chocolate is important for successful dipping (see above).
● Do not let any water fall into the chocolate – it will cause the chocolate to *tighten* or stiffen and spoil the whole batch.
● Before moving dipped chocolates, cool until completely set. The chocolate should be firm.

Getting Ready

At least one day ahead, prepare the various flavours of fondant, creams, crystallised orange peel, caramels, nut fillings or fruit to be used as centres.

If possible, choose a cool, clear day with low humidity for dipping. Moisture in the air can dull your chocolates. The temperature in the room where you are dipping should be between 13 and 20 C/60 to 70 F.

Do not work in an area where the chocolates will be in a draught. If it's necessary to cool the room, open a window in an adjoining room or partially open a window where the draught will not blow on the confectionery.

It is not necessary to dip the sweets at the stove or hob. In fact, it is better to be away from the heat. Although you'll need almost boiling water to start melting chocolate, keep the sweets away from the hot oven or steam from a boiling pot or kettle.

Assemble the equipment. You will need:
● A double boiler or bowl that will fit in a pan without its bottom touching the hot water.
● A spoon or rubber spatula for stirring.
● A dipping or fondue fork for dipping sweets.
● A thermometer with a range of at least from 27 to 54 C, 80 to 130 F. Some sugar thermometers have this range. You are most likely to find them in specialist kitchen shops.
● A cooling rack covered with waxed paper or foil.

Have the sweet centres ready; place them near the dipping equipment. If you are dipping cherries, dip them into the fondant and let stand while melting the chocolate. Form or cut other sweet centres into desired shapes.

Now you are ready. The two following methods have been fully tested. Follow them carefully and they should give good results.

Plain Fondant

A basic fondant for Fondant Cherries, page 61, or for chocolate dipped centres.

450 g/1 lb sugar
175 m/6 fl oz water
1 tablespoon golden syrup
⅛ teaspoon salt
1 teaspoon vanilla essence

If you don't have a marble surface to work on, chill a 38 × 23-cm/15 × 9-in baking tray in the refrigerator. In a 2.25-litre/2-quart saucepan, combine the sugar, water, golden syrup and salt. Stir constantly over medium heat until the sugar dissolves and the mixture boils. Cover and cook over low heat for 3 minutes. Uncover. Insert a sugar thermometer in the mixture. Continue cooking without stirring until the mixture reaches 115 C, 240 F or soft-ball stage. Remove from the heat and pour onto a clean and dry marble surface or chilled baking tray. Cool without stirring until the centre of the fondant is lukewarm. With a spatula or wooden spoon, scrape the fondant from the edge towards the centre, turning occasionally, until creamy and stiff. When the fondant loses its gloss and becomes crumbly, knead with your hands until smooth and soft. At first, kneading will seem impossible but the heat from your hands will soften the fondant. Add the vanilla and continue kneading until blended. Wrap in cling film and refrigerate in a covered container for at least 24 hours. **Makes 40 to 45 centres for dipping.**

Cream Fondant

Rich creamy fondant in two delectable flavours for dipping into chocolate.

450 g/1 lb sugar
3 tablespoons hot water
175 ml/6 fl oz whipping cream
2 tablespoons golden syrup
15 g/$\frac{1}{2}$ butter
$\frac{1}{2}$ teaspoon vanilla essence
$\frac{1}{8}$ teaspoon peppermint essence
4 drops red food colouring
$\frac{1}{2}$ teaspoon grated orange rind
25 g/1 oz desiccated coconut
4 drops orange food colouring

If you do not have a marble surface to work on, chill a 38 × 23-cm/15 × 9-in baking tray in the refrigerator. In a 2.25-litre/2-quart saucepan, combine the sugar, hot water, cream and golden syrup. Stir constantly over medium heat until the mixture boils. Reduce the heat to low, cover and cook for 3 minutes. Remove the cover and continue cooking without stirring until the mixture reaches 115 C, 240 F on a sugar thermometer, or soft-ball stage. Remove from the heat and, without scraping the pan, immediately pour the mixture onto a clean and dry marble surface or chilled baking tray. Dot the top with butter but do not stir. Cool until the centre is lukewarm. With a spatula or wooden spoon, scrape the fondant from the edge towards the centre, turning occasionally, until creamy and stiff. When the mixture loses its gloss and becomes crumbly, knead with your hands until smooth and soft. As you begin, kneading will seem impossible, but the heat from your hands will soften the mixture. Add the vanilla and continue kneading until blended. Wrap in cling film and refrigerate for 24 hours in a covered container. When ready to dip into the chocolate, divide the fondant in half. Knead the peppermint extract and red food colouring into one half, then knead the orange peel, coconut and orange food colouring into the other half. Form each half into a roll 2.5 cm/1 in in diameter. Slice the rolls 1 cm/$\frac{1}{2}$ in thick. For variety, form some slices into cubes and ovals. Place on waxed paper. Cover and let stand for several hours at room temperature before dipping into chocolate. **Makes 45 to 50 centres.**

Dipping With Plain Chocolate

450 g/1 lb plain chocolate
70 to 80 centres, pages 58 to 61
nuts or raisins, as desired

1. Unwrap the chocolate and chop it finely. Place in the top of a double boiler.
2. Pour amost boiling water about 5 cm/2 in deep into the bottom of a double boiler. The water should not touch the bottom of the top part of the double boiler.
3. Place the top of the double boiler with the chocolate over hot water. Do not place the double boiler on heating unit.
4. Stir the chocolate constantly until melted so it will melt evenly.
5. Insert the thermometer in the melted chocolate. Continue stirring vigorously until the temperature reaches 54 C, 130 F. Remove the top of the double boiler from the hot water.
6. Pour hot water from the bottom of the double boiler. Replace with cold tap water. Place the top of the double boiler with melted chocolate over cold water. Stir and scrape the side of the pan with a spoon or spatula until the temperature of the chocolate is 28 C, 83 F. If necessary, replace the cold water in the bottom of the double boiler once or twice.
7. Maintain the chocolate at 28 C, 83 F, which is the recommended dipping temperature for plain chocolate pieces. Replace the water in the bottom of the double boiler with slightly warmer or cooler water as needed during the dipping.
8. Drop 1 centre into the chocolate. Stir with a fork. Slip the fork under the coated centre and lift out quickly. Rap the fork on the edge of the pan several times, then draw the fork and centre across the rim of the pan to remove excess chocolate.
9. Invert the dipped centre on waxed paper or a foil-covered wire rack. As the fork is removed, a thread of chocolate will fall across the top of the sweet to form a design. Expert sweet dippers form a different design for each flavour to identify varieties.
10. Continue to stir the melted chocolate as often as possible during the dipping process. Work quickly and check the temperature of the chocolate frequently.
11. When there's very little chocolate left in the pan, drop in small items such as nuts or raisins. Stir until well-coated. Pick up in clusters with a spoon and drop on waxed paper or foil on a wire rack.
12. Cool the chocolates until set. **Makes 70 to 80.**

Dipping Chocolates

1 Place the chocolate in the top of a double boiler over *very* hot water in the bottom of the double boiler.

2 To check the temperature, insert a thermometer into the chocolate and attach it to the side of the pan.

3 While melting chocolate and dipping sweets, stir the chocolate as much as possible to maintain an even temperature.

4 When the chocolate reaches the correct dipping temperature, drop in a sweet centre. Lift out with a fork.

Dipping with Milk and Plain Chocolate

175 g/6 oz milk chocolate, broken into pieces
175 g/6 oz plain chocolate, broken into pieces
50 to 60 centres, pages 58 to 61
nuts or raisins, as desired

1. Place milk chocolate pieces and plain chocolate pieces in the top of a double boiler.
2. Pour almost boiling water about 5 cm/2 in deep into the bottom of the double boiler. The hot water should not touch the bottom of the top part of the double boiler.
3. Place the top of the double boiler with the chocolate over hot water. Do not place the double boiler on the heat.
4. Stir the chocolate constantly until melted so it will melt evenly.
5. Insert a thermometer in the melted chocolate. Continue to stir vigorously until the temperature reaches 42 c, 108 f. Immediately remove the top of the double boiler from the bottom pan of hot water.
6. Pour the hot water from the bottom of the double boiler and replace it with cold tap water. Place the top of the double boiler with the melted chocolate over cold water. Stir and scrape the side of the pan with a spoon or spatula until the temperature is 27 c, 80 f. If necessary, replace the cold water in the bottom of the double boiler once or twice. Keep the chocolate at 27 c, 80 f for 5 minutes, stirring vigorously. Remove from the cold water.
7. Pour the cold water from the bottom of the double boiler. Replace with warm water, 32 c, 90 f to 35 c, 95 f. Place the top of the double boiler with the chocolate over warm water. Stir constantly until the chocolate warms to 30 c, 86 f. This is the recommended dipping temperature for the combination of milk chocolate pieces with plain pieces. Maintain this temperature throughout dipping. If necessary, replace the water in the bottom of the double boiler with slightly warmer or cooler water.
8. Drop 1 centre into the chocolate. Stir well with a fork. Slip the fork under the coated centre and lift out quickly. Rap the fork on the edge of the pan several times, then draw both fork and centre across the rim of the pan to remove excess chocolate.
9. Invert the dipped centre onto waxed paper or a foil-covered wire rack. As the fork is removed, a thread of chocolate will fall across the top of the sweet to form a design. Expert sweet dippers form a different design for each flavour of candy to identify varieties.

10. Continue to stir the melted chocolate as often as possible during the dipping process. Work quickly and check the temperature of the chocolate frequently.
11. When there is very little chocolate left in the pan, drop in small items such as nuts or raisins. Stir until well-coated. Pick up in clusters with a spoon. Drop on waxed paper or foil on a wire rack.
12. Cool the chocolates until set. **Makes 50 to 60.**

Chocolate-tipped Orange Peels

Prepare the orange peel 24 hours before dipping.

2 medium oranges
175 g/6 oz golden syrup
225 g/8 oz sugar
250 ml/8 fl oz water
sugar for coating the orange peels
chocolate for dipping, (page 56)

With a knife, score the peel of the orange into 6 sections. Remove the peel from the oranges in scored sections. In a medium-sized saucepan, cover the peel with water. Heat to boiling and boil for 10 minutes. Drain. Repeat, covering with water, boiling and draining 2 more times. After each cooking period, gently scrape off some of the soft white membrane with a spoon. Cut the peel into strips about 5 mm/$\frac{1}{4}$ in wide. Combine the golden syrup, sugar and water in a 2.25-litre/2-quart saucepan. Stir constantly over medium heat until the sugar dissolves. Add strips of orange peel and bring to a boil, then simmer for 45 minutes. Drain and cool. Roll the strips in sugar and arrange in a single layer on baking sheets. Let stand at room temperature for about 24 hours before dipping. Picking up a few orange strips in your fingers, dip the ends only into melted chocolate. Place on a baking sheet to harden. **Makes 45 to 50 pieces.**

Fondant Cherries

A few days' standing time gives the fondant and cherries a chance to create the delicious liquid layer.

1 (255 g/8 oz) jar maraschino cherries, with stems if possible
½ recipe Plain Fondant (page 57)
chocolate for dipping (page 56)

Drain the cherry juice and place the cherries on kitchen paper. Melt the fondant in the top of a double boiler over hot water until it becomes a thick syrup. Place a sheet of waxed paper on the working surface. Dip the drained cherries one at a time into the fondant syrup, completely covering each cherry. Place on waxed paper to cool. When the syrup-covered cherries are completely cooled, prepare the chocolate for dipping. Dip the bottom half of each cherry into chocolate. Return to the waxed paper and let harden. Line a tray or baking sheet with waxed paper. When the chocolate on the cherries has cooled and hardened, dip again; this time completely coat each cherry with chocolate. Cool on the prepared tray or baking sheet. Stand in a cool dry place for a few days. **Makes about 30 fondant cherries.**

Brown Sugar Operas

Brown sugar squares make delicious centres for dipped chocolates

225 g/8 oz granulated sugar
225 g/8 oz soft brown sugar
1 tablespoon golden syrup
150 ml/¼ pint condensed milk
250 ml/8 fl oz whole milk
½ teaspoon vanilla essence

Butter a 20-cm/8-in square tin; set aside. In a heavy 2.25-litre/2-quart saucepan, combine the granulated and brown sugars. Stir in the golden syrup, condensed milk and whole milk. Bring to a boil and cook, stirring constantly, until the mixture reaches 112 C, 234 F on a sugar thermometer, or soft-ball stage. Stir in the vanilla. Cool to lukewarm then beat until the mixture is creamy, has thickened and is no longer glossy. Pour into the prepared tin. Cool, then cut into squares. **Makes 36 centres for dipping.**

Peanut Butter Squares

Crunchy squares give a new shape and texture to dipped chocolate.

50 g/2 oz butter
50 g/2 oz chunky peanut butter
175 g/6 oz golden syrup
1 tablespoon water
1 teaspoon vanilla essence
450 g/1 lb icing sugar
25 g/1 oz dried milk powder

Butter a 20-cm/8-in square tin and set it aside. In the top of a double boiler over boiling water, combine the butter and peanut butter and stir until the butter melts. Add the golden syrup, water and vanilla and mix well. Combine the icing sugar and dried milk. Gradually stir the sugar mixture into the peanut butter mixture. Heat over boiling water until smooth. Pour into the prepared tin and leave to cool before cutting into squares. **Makes 36 centres for dipping.**

Butterscotch and Walnut Squares

You won't be able to resist nibbling these praline-flavoured confections while dipping.

225 g/8 oz brown sugar
50 g/2 oz butter
3 tablespoons milk
225 g/8 oz sifted icing sugar
25 g/1 oz chopped walnuts
1 teaspoon vanilla essence

Butter a 20-cm/8-inch square tin and set it aside. In a 2.25-litre/2-quart saucepan, combine the brown sugar, butter and milk. Bring to a boil, stirring constantly, then simmer for 5 minutes. Remove from the heat and stir in the icing sugar, walnuts and vanilla. Pour into the prepared tin. Cool. When firm, cut into squares. **Makes 45 to 50 centres for dipping.**

Creamy Rich Fudge

Exceptionally creamy fudge with a strong chocolate flavour

100 g/4 oz plain chocolate
300 ml/½ pint milk
675 g/1½ lb sugar
2 tablespoons golden syrup
⅛ teaspoon salt
50 g/2 oz butter or margarine
1 teaspoon vanilla essence
50 g/2 oz chopped nuts

Lightly butter a 20-cm/8-in square tin; set aside. In a 3.5-litre/3-quart saucepan, constantly stir the chocolate and milk over low heat until the chocolate melts. Stir in the sugar, golden syrup and salt. Cook, stirring occasionally, until the mixture reaches soft-ball stage or 113 C, 236 F, on a sugar thermometer. Remove from the heat and add the butter or margarine. Cool at room temperature without stirring until the temperature drops to 48 C, 120 F or the bottom of the pan feels warm, about 1 hour. Add the vanilla and beat until the fudge mixture loses its gloss and starts to thicken. Quickly stir in the nuts then pour into the prepared tin. Cool until firm. Cut into squares. **Makes 36 pieces.**

Rocky Road Fudge

Delicious fudge with all kinds of goodies mixed in.

675 g/1½ lb sugar
75 g/3 oz unsweetened cocoa powder
175 g/6 oz golden syrup
300 ml/½ pint milk
50 g/2 oz butter or margarine
1 teaspoon vanilla essence
100 g/4 oz glacé cherries, halved
175 g/6 oz marshmallows, chopped
50 g/2 oz coarsely chopped nuts
75 g/2 oz desiccated coconut

Lightly butter a 33 × 23-cm/13 × 9-in baking tin. In a 3.5-litre/3-quart saucepan, combine the sugar, cocoa, golden syrup and milk. Cook over moderate heat until the sugar dissolves and the mixture begins to boil. Continue cooking over medium-low heat, stirring occasionally, until the mixture reaches soft-ball stage or 114 C, 238 F on a sugar thermometer. Remove from the heat. Add the butter or margarine and vanilla, but do not stir. Cool to lukewarm, then beat until creamy. Stir in the glacé cherries, marshmallows, nuts and coconut. Pour into the prepared tin. Cut into squares when cool. **Makes about 50 squares.**

Rocky Road Fudge

Pronto Fudge

Marshmallow cream fudge is quick, easy and creamy with a subtle chocolate flavour.

100 g/4 oz butter or margarine
675 g/1½ lb sugar
1 (170-g/6-oz) can evaporated milk, not diluted
350 g/12 oz plain chocolate, broken into pieces
200 g/7 oz marshmallows, chopped finely
50 g/2 oz chopped nuts
1 teaspoon vanilla essence

Lightly butter a 33 × 23-cm/13 × 9-in tin. In a heavy 3 or 3.5-litre/2½ or 3-quart saucepan, melt the butter or margarine over low heat. Add the sugar and evaporated milk. Stirring constantly, bring to a rolling boil over medium-low heat. Cook, stirring constantly, for about 4 minutes or until the mixture reaches 108 C, 226 F, on a sugar thermometer. Remove from the heat and add the chocolate pieces. Beat with a spoon until melted. Stir in the finely chopped marshmallows, nuts and vanilla. Pour into the prepared tin. Cool, then cut into squares. **Makes about 60 pieces.**

No-work Fudge

For those who like rich dark chocolate the easy way.

450 g/1 lb plain chocolate, broken into pieces
1 (397-g/14-oz) can sweetened condensed milk
1 teaspoon vanilla essence
50 g/2 oz chopped walnuts

Butter a 20-cm/8-in square tin and set it aside. In a 2.25-litre/2-quart saucepan, melt the chocolate pieces. Stir in the condensed milk, vanilla and walnuts. Pour into the prepared tin. Refrigerate for about 2 hours or until firm, then cut into squares. **Makes about 25 squares.**

Peanut Butter Chip Fudge

Peanut butter pieces partially melted in milk chocolate fudge create a swirled effect.

450 g/1 lb granulated sugar
225 g/8 oz demerara or soft brown sugar
175 g/6 oz milk chocolate, broken into pieces
300 ml/½ pint milk
2 tablespoons golden syrup
25 g/1 oz butter or margarine
1 teaspoon vanilla essence
175 g/6 oz peanut butter

Lightly butter a 20-cm/8-in square tin; set aside. In a 3.5-litre/3-quart pan, combine the granulated and brown sugars, chocolate pieces, milk and golden syrup. Bring to a boil, stirring until the sugar dissolves. Cook over medium heat without stirring until the mixture reaches the soft-ball stage, 113 C, 236 F on a sugar thermometer. Remove from the heat and add the butter or margarine. Let cool without stirring until the bottom of pan feels warm, about 48 C, 120 F. Add the vanilla and beat until the fudge thickens and begins to lose its gloss. Quickly stir in the peanut butter. Pour into the prepared tin and cool until firm. Cut into squares. **Makes about 36 pieces.**

Peanut Butter Fudge

1 kg/2 lb sugar
1 teaspoon salt
50 g/2 oz unsweetened cocoa powder
350 ml/12 fl oz milk
50 g/2 oz butter or margarine
2 teaspoons vanilla essence
175 g/6 oz peanut butter

Butter a 28 × 18-cm/11 × 7-in tin; set aside. In a 3.5-litre/3-quart saucepan, combine the sugar, salt and cocoa. Add the milk and stir until blended. Cook over medium-to-low heat, stirring occasionally, until the sugar just dissolves. Add the butter or margarine and continue cooking without stirring until the mixture reaches the soft-ball stage or 114 C, 238 F on a sugar thermometer. Remove from the heat and cool at room temperature without stirring until the bottom of the pan is warm, about 48 C, 120 F. Add the vanilla and peanut butter. Beat until the fudge mixture loses its gloss and begins to thicken. Pour into the prepared tin. Cool until firm. Cut into squares. **Makes 35 pieces.**

Whisky Balls

175 g/6 oz plain chocolate, broken into pieces
3 tablespoons golden syrup
3 tablespoons whisky
75 g/3 oz sugar
50 g/2 oz ice cream wafer crumbs
100 g/4 oz finely chopped walnuts
icing sugar

Melt the chocolate. Stir in the golden syrup, whisky, sugar, ice cream wafer crumbs and walnuts. Using a heaped teaspoon of mixture for each piece, form into balls; roll in icing sugar. Cover and refrigerate for several hours. **Makes about 36 balls.**

Traditional English Toffee

Crunchy toffee with a chocolate-nut topping.

225 g/8 oz butter or margarine
175 g/6 oz sugar
2 tablespoons water
1 tablespoon golden syrup
100 g/4 oz chopped walnuts
100 g/4 oz cooking chocolate

Lightly butter a baking tray and set it aside. In a 2.25-litre/2-quart saucepan, melt the butter or margarine. Add the sugar, water and golden syrup. Cook over low heat, stirring occasionally, until the mixture reaches the soft-crack stage or 143 C, 290 F on a sugar thermometer. Remove from the heat and quickly add 50 g/2 oz of the chopped walnuts. Spread about 5 mm/$\frac{1}{4}$ in thick on the prepared baking tray. Cool thoroughly. Melt the chocolate and allow to cool slightly, then spread over the cooled toffee. Sprinkle with the remaining chopped walnuts. Refrigerate until firm. Break into small pieces. **Makes 50 to 60 pieces.**

Oasis Bonbons

100 g/4 oz plain chocolate
175 g/6 oz crunchy peanut butter
100 g/4 oz icing sugar
50 g/2 oz desiccated coconut
225 g/8 oz chopped stoned dates
1 teaspoon grated orange rind

Line a baking tray with waxed paper; set aside. Melt the chocolate and set it aside also. In a medium-sized bowl, combine the peanut butter, icing sugar, coconut, dates and orange rind. Shape into 2.5-cm/1-in balls. Dip the top half of each ball into melted chocolate. Place on the prepared baking tray with the chocolate side up. Chill until the chocolate is set. **Makes about 35 bonbons.**

How to make Mint Truffles

1 To make the chocolate melt faster, coarsely chop both kinds before combining in the double boiler. Stir the chocolate occasionally until it is melted and smooth.

2 Small (3-cm/1½-in) petits fours cases are just right for this job. With a clean, dry brush, carefully coat the inside of each paper case with the melted chocolate. It will be difficult to peel off the paper later if you go over the top edge. Chill the chocolate cups while you make the filling.

3 The filling is made of more chocolate with butter and eggs plus peppermint flavouring. When the mixture looks like chocolate-coloured mayonnaise, it's time to fill the chilled cups. Spoon about one rounded teaspoonful of mixture into each cup.

4 After the cases are filled, cover and refrigerate until serving time. They may be frozen for longer storage. While they are still cold, carefully peel off the paper and serve.

Mint Truffles

You'll need 36 petits fours cases and a 1-cm/½-in brush.

175 g/6 oz plain cooking chocolate
1 (approx 225 g/8 oz) bar of milk chocolate, halved
100 g/4 oz butter or margarine
3 eggs
⅛ teaspoon salt
½ teaspoon peppermint essence

Coarsely chop 50 g/2 oz of the plain cooking chocolate and half the bar of milk chocolate. Combine in the top of a double boiler over hot but not simmering water. Stir occasionally until melted and smooth. Loosen the top petit four case from the stack, but leave in the stack for greater stability while being coated. With a small, clean and dry paintbrush, coat the inside of the top cup evenly with melted chocolate, about 2 to 3 mm/1/16 to ⅛ in thick, bringing the coating almost to the top of each case but not over the edge. Carefully remove the coated cup from the stack. Repeat until the 36 cases are coated, stirring the chocolate occasionally while you work. Refrigerate the coated cases. Coarsely chop the remaining half of the milk chocolate bar and the rest of the cooking chocolate. In a small saucepan, melt the butter or margarine until it bubbles and foams. Remove from the heat, add the chopped chocolate and stir until melted and smooth. In a small bowl, beat the eggs and salt until foamy and pale yellow in colour. With an electric mixer on high speed, very gradually add the warm chocolate mixture. The mixture should be about the thickness of mayonnaise. Stir in the peppermint essence. Drop by rounded teaspoonfuls into the chocolate cups. Arrange a single layer of filled cups in a 2-cm/¾-in deep tin or plastic container. Cover and refrigerate or freeze. To serve, peel off the paper cases while the truffles are cold or frozen. Arrange in a single layer on a serving dish. **Makes about 36 pieces.**

Two-tone Mint Divinities

Each piece has a chocolate layer and a mint divinity layer.

25 g/1 oz plain chocolate
350 g/12 oz sugar
100 g/4 oz golden syrup
4 tablespoons water
2 egg whites
½ teaspoon vanilla essence
50 g/2 oz finely crushed peppermint rock

Melt the chocolate and set it aside. Lightly butter a 23 × 13-cm/9 × 5-in loaf tin. In a 2.25-litre/2-quart saucepan, combine the sugar, golden syrup and water. Bring to a boil, stirring until the sugar dissolves. Boil over a moderate heat without stirring until the mixture reaches the soft-ball stage or 113 C, 236 F on a sugar thermometer. While the mixture is boiling, beat the egg whites in a large bowl until stiff peaks form. Pour the hot syrup very slowly over the beaten egg whites, beating until the mixture forms soft peaks. Pour half of the mixture into another bowl. To the remaining mixture add the melted chocolate and vanilla. Spoon into the prepared tin. Add the crushed peppermint rock to the other half of the mixture. Spoon over the chocolate layer and cool until set. Cut into squares. **Makes about 32 squares.**

Quick Mint Drops

Favourites for parties and after dinner.

40 g/1½ oz butter or margarine
3 tablespoons milk
450 g/1 lb chocolate flavour icing mix
½ teaspoon peppermint essence

Melt the butter or margarine with the milk in the top of a double boiler. Stir in the icing mix and cook over rapidly boiling water for 5 minutes, stirring occasionally. Stir in the peppermint. Drop from a teaspoon onto waxed paper and swirl the tops of the sweets with a spoon. If the mixture becomes too thick, add a few drops of hot water. Cool the mint drops until firm. **Makes about 60.**

Quick French Creams

225 g/8 oz cooking chocolate
175 g/6 oz sifted icing sugar
1 tablespoon milk
1 egg, well beaten
50 g/2 oz chocolate vermicelli

In the top of a double boiler over hot but not simmering water, melt the chocolate, stirring until smooth. Remove from the water and quickly stir in the icing sugar, milk and egg. Refrigerate until firm enough to shape. Form into 2.5-cm/1-in balls. Roll in the chocolate vermicelli. **Makes 35 to 40 balls.**

Peanut Crisp

Peanuts, chocolate, marshmallow and Rice Krispies make a super afternoon snack.

100 g/4 oz butter or margarine
175 g/6 oz peanut butter
350 g/12 oz milk chocolate drops
150 g/5 oz marshmallows
100 g/4 oz Rice Krispies
200 g/7 oz unsalted peanuts

Lightly butter a 33 × 23-cm/13 × 9-in shallow baking tray; set aside. In a 3.5-litre/3-quart saucepan, combine the butter or margarine, peanut butter and half the chocolate drops. Stir constantly over low heat until the chocolate melts. Add the marshmallows, stirring until melted, then stir in the Rice Krispies and peanuts. Immediately pat the mixture into the prepared tin and sprinkle with the remaining chocolate drops. Cover the tin with foil and let stand for several minutes or until the chocolate starts to melt. With a small spatula, smooth the chocolate over the top. Refrigerate until set. Cut into bars. **Makes about 36 bars.**

Cocoa Pralines

450 g/1 lb soft brown sugar
1 tablespoon unsweetened cocoa powder
⅛ teaspoon salt
150 ml/¼ pint evaporated milk
2 tablespoons butter or margarine
175 g/6 oz whole pecans

Lightly butter a baking tray or large piece of aluminium foil. In a 2.25-litre/2-quart saucepan, combine the brown sugar, cocoa, salt, evaporated milk and butter or margarine. Stir constantly over low heat until the sugar dissolves. Add the pecans then stir constantly over a medium heat, until the mixture reaches soft-ball stage or 112 C, 234 F on a sugar thermometer. Remove from the heat; cool for 5 minutes. Stir until the mixture begins to thicken and coats the pecans. Drop from a teaspoon onto the prepared baking tray or foil, forming fairly flat round sweets about 3.5–5 cm/1½–2 in in diameter. If the praline mixture stiffens too much in the saucepan, add a few drops of hot water. **Makes about 30 pralines.**

Butter-nut Crunch

These are crunchy, yet melt in your mouth.
Illustrated on page 54

175 g/6 oz sugar
½ teaspoon salt
100 g/4 oz butter or margarine
50 ml/2 fl oz water
100 g/4 oz chopped walnuts
450 g/1 lb plain chocolate, broken into pieces

Butter a 38 × 25-cm/15 × 10-in baking tray; set aside. In a medium-sized saucepan, combine the sugar, salt, butter or margarine and water. Cook until mixture reaches soft-crack stage or 132 C, 270 F on a sugar thermometer. Stir in half the chopped walnuts. Pour onto the prepared baking tray. If necessary, spread to about ½-cm/¼-in thickness. Cool. Melt chocolate and spread it over. Sprinkle with the remaining chopped walnuts. When cool, break into irregular chunks. **Makes 35 to 40 pieces.**

Pecan or Walnut Penuche

An ever-popular penuche with a chocolate topping.

450 g/1 lb granulated sugar
400 g/14 oz demerara or soft brown sugar
100 ml/4 fl oz single cream
150 ml/¼ pint milk
40 g/1½ oz butter or margarine
1½ teaspoons vanilla essence
100 g/4 oz coarsely chopped pecans or walnuts
175 g/6 oz plain chocolate, broken into pieces
about 24 pecan or walnut halves

Butter a 20-cm/8-in square baking tin; set aside. Butter a 3 or 3.5-litre/2½ or 3-quart saucepan. Add the granulated and brown sugars, cream, milk and butter or margarine. Cook over medium heat, stirring until the sugar just dissolves and the mixture boils. Boil without stirring until the mixture reaches soft-ball stage or 113 C, 236 F on a sugar thermometer. Remove from the heat. Cool without stirring until the bottom of the pan is warm, or to 50 C, 120 F. Add the vanilla. With the electric mixer on high speed, beat until the mixture thickens and begins to lose its gloss. Quickly stir in the chopped pecans or walnuts and pour into the prepared tin, spreading it evenly over the bottom. While still warm but firm, cut into 24 pieces. Cool in the pan. When the penuche in the pan is cool, melt the chocolate pieces and spoon the melted chocolate in a zig-zag pattern over the top of the sweets. Place a pecan or walnut half on top of each piece. **Makes about 24.**

Mocha Pecan Logs

Dark chocolate with a hint of coffee.

175 g/6 oz demerara or soft brown sugar
4 tablespoons evaporated milk
2 tablespoons golden syrup
175 g/6 oz plain chocolate, broken into pieces
1 teaspoons instant coffee powder
1 teaspoon vanilla essence
100 g/4 oz chopped pecans or walnuts

Grease a large baking tray and set it aside. In a heavy, medium-sized saucepan, combine the sugar, milk and golden syrup. Bring to a boil over medium heat, stirring constantly. Boil and stir for 2 minutes. Remove from the heat, add the chocolate pieces, coffee and vanilla, stirring until the chocolate melts. With a wooden spoon, beat until thick and smooth. Stir in the pecans or walnuts. Spoon onto the prepared baking tray in 2 equal parts. Shape each half into a 25-cm/10-in long log. Wrap each log in waxed paper. Refrigerate for about 2 hours or until firm. Cut each log into 20 pieces. **Makes 40 pieces.**

Peanut Butter and Oatmeal Drops

Children love these quick-to-make drops.

450 g/1 lb sugar
25 g/1 oz unsweetened cocoa powder
150 ml/¼ pint milk
50 g/2 oz butter
75 g/3 oz crunchy peanut butter
1 teaspoon vanilla essence
275 g/10 oz uncooked quick-cooking rolled oats

Line a baking tray with waxed paper and set it aside. In a medium-sized saucepan, combine the sugar and cocoa. Stir in the milk and butter. Bring to a boil over medium heat, stirring constantly. Simmer for about 2 minutes then remove from heat. Stir in the peanut butter and vanilla, then the oats. Drop from a teaspoon onto the waxed paper. Cool until firm. **Makes 38 to 46 pieces.**

Creamy Desserts

The recipes in this chapter are based on delectable blends of chocolate with eggs and milk or cream. They range in variety and simplicity from plain Baked Cocoa Custard to elegant Charlotte Russe. Some are baked while others are either steamed or cooked in a saucepan.

When steaming a pudding, be sure to cover the basin or mould. If it does not have a lid that clamps on, cover with foil and tie tightly with a string. Place the mould on a metal rack in a large saucepan or steamer and pour water around the mould. Cover the pan so the heated water will steam the pudding. Steam cooking is a slow method, so allow several hours for this process.

Stirred puddings and custards, those cooked in a saucepan, are usually a custard mixture with different flavourings. The more elaborate ones include whipped cream, gelatine, nuts and liqueurs for a glamorous look and taste. For a smooth texture, keep the heat low and stir the chocolate mixtures while they are cooking. Neither eggs nor chocolate cook well at high temperatures, so if your custard mixture looks slightly grainy or if chocolate flecks remain, beat it with a wire whisk or rotary beater. Naturally, all dishes made with eggs or milk products should be kept in the refrigerator until serving time.

Floating Islands (page 74)

Steamed Fudge Pudding

75 g/3 oz plain chocolate
25 g/1 oz butter or margarine, softened
100 g/4 oz sugar
2 eggs
2 teaspoons baking powder
¼ teaspoon salt
1 teaspoon vanilla essence
225 g/8 oz plain flour
225 ml/8 fl oz milk
50 g/2 oz chopped walnuts
Sugar Cream Sauce (see below)
SUGAR CREAM SAUCE
100 g/4 oz butter or margarine
225 g/8 oz sugar
150 ml/¼ pint single cream
½ teaspoon vanilla essence

Melt the chocolate and set it aside. Grease a 1.75-litre/3-pint mould and set aside also. In a medium-sized bowl, cream the butter or margarine and sugar until light and fluffy. Beat in the eggs and stir in the baking powder, salt and vanilla. Beat in the flour alternately with the milk. Add the melted chocolate and walnuts and stir until blended. Pour into the prepared mould. Cover with foil and press overhanging foil edges against the outside of the mould. Loop a large rubber band over the foil and around the top of the mould to seal, or tie the foil securely with string. Place the mould on a rack in a large pan and pour enough water into the pot to reach halfway up the mould. Cover the pot and bring to a boil; simmer for 1½ hours or until a skewer inserted in the pudding comes out clean. Remove the mould from the pan. Cool on a wire rack for 10 minutes. Meanwhile prepare the Sugar Cream Sauce. Unmould the pudding, and spoon the sauce over the warm pudding. **Serves 8 to 10.**

Sugar Cream Sauce

Combine the butter or margarine, sugar, cream and vanilla in a medium-sized saucepan. Heat to boiling point.

Steamed Date Pudding

75 g/3 oz butter or margarine, softened
225 g/8 oz demerara or soft brown sugar
2 eggs
2 tablespoons unsweetened cocoa powder
1 teaspoon bicarbonate of soda
175 g/6 oz plain flour
225 ml/8 fl oz water
175 g/6 oz plain chocolate drops
175 g/6 oz finely chopped stoned dates
50 g/2 oz chopped walnuts
1 teaspoon grated orange rind

Grease and flour a 1.75-litre/3-pint mould; set aside. In a large bowl, cream the butter or margarine and brown sugar. Beat in the eggs, then the cocoa and bicarbonate of soda. Add the flour alternately with the water, beating after each addition. With a spoon, stir in the chocolate drops, dates, walnuts and orange rind. Pour into the prepared mould, cover with foil and press the overhanging foil edges against the outside of the mould. Loop a large rubber band over the foil and around the top of the mould to seal, or tie the foil securely with string. Place the mould on a rack in a large pan and pour enough boiling water into the pan to reach halfway up the mould. Cover the pan and simmer for about 2 hours or until a skewer inserted into the pudding comes out clean. Remove the mould from the pan. Let stand 15 minutes. Loosen the edges with a knife and invert onto a serving platter. Serve warm. **Serves 8 to 10.**

Fudge-top Pudding

A light delicate cake on top with rich fudge sauce on the bottom.

100 g/4 oz plain flour
175 g/6 oz granulated sugar
40 g/1½ oz unsweetened cocoa powder
2 teaspoons baking powder
¼ teaspoon salt
100 ml/4 fl oz milk
2 tablespoons cooking oil
50 g/2 oz chopped walnuts
225 g/8 oz soft brown sugar
450 ml/¾ pint hot water
whipped cream, if desired

Set the oven at 180 C, 350 F, gas 4. In a medium-sized bowl, combine the flour, granulated sugar, 2 tablespoons of the cocoa, baking powder and salt. Add the milk and oil and stir until smooth. Stir in the walnuts and pour into an ungreased 23-cm/9-in square tin. Combine the brown sugar and the remaining cocoa and sprinkle over the batter. Pour hot water over all, but *do not stir*. Bake for 40 to 45 minutes; the pudding will be done when the topping begins to leave the sides of the tin although the centre may not appear firm. Serve warm. Spoon the cake-like top upside down into dessert dishes and spoon the sauce from the bottom of the tin over each serving. Top with whipped cream, if desired. **Serves 8 or 9.**

Charlotte Russe

This is light and airy, yet rich with chocolate.

225 g/8 oz sugar
15 g/½ oz powdered gelatine
75 g/3 oz plain chocolate
475 ml/16 fl oz milk
4 egg yolks, slightly beaten
3 tablespoons rum
15 sponge fingers, split lengthways
4 egg whites
300 ml/½ pint whipping cream
additional whipped cream, if desired

In a small saucepan, combine the sugar and gelatine. Add the chocolate. Stir in the milk and egg yolks then stir constantly over low heat until smooth and slightly thickened. If flecks of chocolate remain, beat with a whisk or electric beater. Pour into a large bowl and refrigerate, stirring occasionally, until the gelatine begins to set. Sprinkle rum on the sponge fingers; stand about 18 sponge finger halves upright around the side of 20-cm/8-in springform tin. In a large bowl, beat the egg whites until stiff but not dry. Whip the cream in a medium-sized bowl. Fold the egg whites into the cooled chocolate mixture, then fold in the whipped cream. Spoon half the mixture into the pan lined with sponge fingers and arrange the remaining 12 sponge finger halves over the filling in the mould. Top with the remaining filling. Chill until firm then unmould and decorate with additional whipped cream, if desired. **Serves 8 to 10.**

Floating Islands

Divine, cloud-like meringues on heavenly chocolate custard.
Illustrated on page 70

3 egg whites
225 g/8 oz sugar
600 ml/1 pint milk
3 egg yolks
2 tablespoons unsweetened cocoa powder
generous pinch of nutmeg
grated chocolate, if desired

In a small bowl, beat the egg whites until foamy. Gradually beat in 175 g/6 oz of the sugar until the meringue is stiff but not dry. In a wide shallow pan over low heat, bring the milk to a simmer. With a large spoon, scoop the meringue into 5 egg-shaped puffs. Gently drop them one at a time into the hot milk. Cover and cook over very low heat for 5 minutes, then lift out with a slotted spoon. Drain on paper towels; chill. Remove the milk from the heat; set aside. In a small bowl, beat the egg yolks until thickened and pale yellow in colour. Gradually add the rest of the sugar. Beat in the cocoa and nutmeg. Strain the milk from the pan onto the egg yolk mixture and mix until blended then pour the blended mixture back into the pan. Stir constantly over low heat until the mixture thickens slightly. Pour into a large shallow serving bowl. Chill. Just before serving, float the meringues on top of the chocolate custard. Sprinkle with grated chocolate, if desired. **Serves 5.**

Baked Cocoa Custard

3 eggs, slightly beaten
175 g/6 oz sugar
1 teaspoon vanilla essence
2 tablespoons unsweetened cocoa powder
600 ml/1 pint milk
nutmeg

Set the oven at 180 C, 350 F, gas 4. In a medium-sized bowl, combine the eggs, sugar, vanilla and cocoa. Stir in the milk. Pour into six 175-ml/6 fl oz custard pots or ramekins. Sprinkle with ground nutmeg and place in a 33 × 23-cm/13 × 9-in baking tin. Pour almost boiling water 2.5 cm/1 in deep into the tin. Bake for 45 minutes or until a skewer or knife inserted into a custard comes out clean. Serve warm or cold. **Serves 6.**

Low-calorie Baked Custard

A really good dessert in spite of its few calories.

60 g/2½ oz sugar
1 tablespoon unsweetened cocoa powder
2 eggs, slightly beaten
½ teaspoon vanilla essence
450 ml/¾ pint skimmed milk
nutmeg

Set the oven at 180 C, 350 F, gas 4. In a medium-sized bowl, combine the sugar and cocoa. Stir in the beaten eggs, vanilla and skim milk. Pour into four 175-ml/6-fl oz ramekins or custard cups. Sprinkle with nutmeg. Place the ramekins or cups in a 28 × 18-cm/11 × 7-in baking tin and pour almost boiling water around them about 2.5 cm/1 in deep. Bake for 45 minutes or until a knife inserted into the custard comes out clean. Serve warm or cold. **Serves 4, about 157 calories per serving.**

Moulded Chocolate Cream

7 whole sponge fingers, split lengthways
100 g/4 oz cooking chocolate
3 tablespoons water
1 teaspoon grated orange rind
1 tablespoon orange liqueur
175 ml/8 fl oz whipping cream
whipped cream, if desired

Line the bottom and sides of a 20 × 10-cm/8 × 4-in loaf tin with foil. Arrange a row of 6 sponge finger halves along the bottom of the tin. Cut the remaining 8 sponge finger halves in half widthways. Stand upright around the sides of the tin. In a small saucepan, combine the chocolate, water and orange rind and stir over low heat until melted. Cool, then stir in the liqueur. Whip the cream in a medium-sized bowl then fold the chocolate mixture into it. Spoon into the sponge finger tin and chill for several hours. To serve, lift from the loaf tin onto a serving plate, peel off the foil and slice. Decorate with whipped cream, if desired. **Serves 6 to 8.**

Pots de Crème au Chocolat

100 g/4 oz plain chocolate
250 ml/8 fl oz whipping cream
3 tablespoons sugar
1 whole egg
2 egg yolks
1 tablespoon vanilla essence
whipped cream, if desired

Set the oven at 180 C, 350 F, gas 4. Break the chocolate into small pieces. Combine the cream and chocolate in a small saucepan and heat over low heat, stirring until the chocolate melts. Stir in the sugar. In a medium bowl, lightly beat the egg and egg yolks together. Add the chocolate mixture gradually, stirring constantly. Stir in the vanilla. Pour into 6 pots de crème pots or custard cups. Cover and set in a 33 × 23-cm/13 × 9-in baking tin. Pour boiling water into the pan halfway up the sides of the pots. Bake on a lower shelf for 15 minutes or until almost firm. Remove the pots from the water and cool. Top with whipped cream if desired. **Serves 6.**

Royal Pots de Crème

These are easy to make and have a truly regal flavour.

100 g/4 oz cooking chocolate
2 tablespoons sugar
150 ml/$\frac{1}{4}$ pint single cream
2 egg yolks, slightly beaten
$\frac{1}{2}$ teaspoon vanilla essence

Break the chocolate into chunks. In a small saucepan over low heat, combine the chocolate, sugar and cream. Stir constantly until smooth. Gradually pour over the beaten egg yolks, beating constantly. Stir in the vanilla and pour into 5 or 6 pots de crème pots or custard cups. Chill. **Serves 4 or 5.**

How to make Pots de Crème au Chocolat

1 This type of Pots de Crème should be cooked like a custard. After adding the chocolate and vanilla, pour the mixture into pots de crème containers or custard pots, then put in a 33 × 23-cm/13 × 9-in baking dish. If the containers have covers, be sure to use them. If not, cover with foil.

2 For best results, pour boiling water into the baking pan. This boiling water starts heating the mixture right away so the baking time is very short. To prevent overcooking, remove the cups from the water as soon as you take them out of the oven.

Easy Pots de Crème

A shortcut version with a hint of coffee.

175 ml/6 fl oz milk
175 g/6 oz plain chocolate, broken into pieces
2 eggs
2 tablespoons strong coffee
1 tablespoon orange liqueur

In a small saucepan, heat the milk until small beads form around the edges but do not allow to boil. In the blender container, combine the chocolate pieces, eggs, coffee and liqueur. Blend until smooth. Add the hot milk and blend again. Pour into 6 or 7 pots de crème pots or custard cups. Chill. **Serves 6 or 7.**

Chocolate Cream Pudding

225 g/8 oz sugar
2 tablespoons cornflour
$\frac{1}{4}$ teaspoon salt
475 ml/16 fl oz milk
50 g/2 oz plain chocolate, cut in small chunks
2 egg yolks, slightly beaten
2 tablespoons butter or margarine
1 teaspoon vanilla essence

In a medium-sized saucepan, combine the sugar, cornflour and salt. Stir in the milk and chocolate. Stir constantly over low heat until thickened and bubbly. Cook and stir 2 minutes more then remove from the heat. Stir a small amount of the hot mixture into the beaten egg yolks, then add the egg yolk mixture to the remaining hot mixture in the saucepan. Cook and stir 2 minutes more. Remove from the heat. Stir in butter or margarine and vanilla. Pour into dessert dishes and chill. **Serves 4 to 6.**

Cocoa Nut Pudding

175 g/6 oz sugar
2 tablespoons cornflour
2 tablespoons unsweetened cocoa powder
generous pinch of salt
475 ml/16 fl oz milk
2 egg yolks, slightly beaten
1 tablespoon butter
1 teaspoon vanilla essence
25 g/1 oz chopped walnuts

In a medium-sized saucepan, combine the sugar, cornflour, cocoa and salt. Stir in the milk and egg yolks. Cook over medium heat until mixture comes to a boil. Simmer for 1 minute longer. Remove from the heat and stir in the butter, vanilla and walnuts. Pour into a serving bowl, cover and cool. **Serves 4 to 5.**

Mousse au Chocolat

This is just about the lightest mousse you've ever tasted.

4 egg yolks, at room temperature
175 g/6 oz sugar
3 tablespoons water
175 g/6 oz plain chocolate, broken into pieces
100 g/4 oz butter
2 tablespoons almond-flavoured liqueur, or rum
4 egg whites, at room temperature
$\frac{1}{4}$ teaspoon cream of tartar

In a small bowl, beat the egg yolks until thickened and pale yellow in colour. Heat the sugar and water in a small saucepan until the mixture begins to boil. Gradually pour the hot mixture over the egg yolks, beating constantly. Heat the chocolate pieces and butter until the chocolate melts. Stir in the liqueur or rum and set aside. Place the bowl with the egg yolk mixture in a pan with almost boiling water and beat for 5 minutes or until doubled in volume. Remove the bowl from the hot water and beat for another 5 minutes. Pour into a large bowl. Fold the chocolate mixture into the egg yolk mixture. In a small bowl, beat the egg whites with the cream of tartar until stiff but not dry, then fold them into the chocolate mixture. Spoon into a large serving bowl or dessert dishes. Refrigerate for several hours. **Serves 8 to 10.**

Royal Velvet Mousse

The smoothest and richest mousse of all.

3 egg yolks, at room temperature
175 g/6 oz sugar
2 tablespoons water
25 g/1 oz plain chocolate
50 g/2 oz milk chocolate
100 g/4 oz butter
2 tablespoons coffee liqueur
3 egg whites, at room temperature
$\frac{1}{4}$ teaspoon cream of tartar
150 ml/$\frac{1}{4}$ pint whipping cream

In a medium-sized bowl, beat the egg yolks until thickened and pale yellow in colour, about 4 minutes. Heat the sugar and water in a small saucepan until the mixture begins to boil. Gradually pour over the egg yolks, beating constantly. Heat the plain and milk chocolate and butter until the chocolate melts. Add the liqueur and set aside. Place the bowl with the egg yolk mixture over a pan of almost boiling water and beat for 5 minutes or until doubled in volume. Remove from the hot water and beat another 5 minutes. Fold the chocolate mixture into the egg yolks. In a small bowl, beat the egg whites with the cream of tartar until stiff but not dry. Fold the beaten egg whites into the chocolate mixture. Beat the whipped cream in a small bowl and fold it into the chocolate mixture. Spoon into a large serving bowl or dessert dishes. Refrigerate or freeze. If frozen, remove from the freezer about 10 minutes before serving. **Serves 6 to 8.**

Orange Mousse

A shortcut mousse made in a blender.

3 egg whites, at room temperature
100 g/4 oz icing sugar
100 g/4 oz plain chocolate, coarsely chopped
3 tablespoons boiling water
3 egg yolks, at room temperature
1 tablespoon orange liqueur
1 teaspoon grated orange rind
whipped cream, if desired

In a medium-sized bowl, beat the egg whites until soft peaks form. Gradually add the icing sugar. Beat until stiff and set aside. In the blender container, combine the chocolate and boiling water and blend until smooth. Add the egg yolks, liqueur and orange peel and blend again until smooth. Fold the chocolate mixture into the beaten egg whites. Spoon into dessert glasses and chill until firm. Decorate with whipped cream, if desired. **Serves 4 or 5.**

Dieter's Chocolate Pudding

175 g/6 oz sugar
2 tablespoons cornflour
2 tablespoons unsweetened cocoa powder
pinch of salt
450 ml/$\frac{3}{4}$ pint skimmed milk
2 egg yolks, slightly beaten
1 teaspoon vanilla essence

In a medium-sized saucepan, combine the sugar, cornflour, cocoa and salt. Stir in the skimmed milk and beaten egg yolks. Stir constantly over medium heat until the mixture comes to a boil; simmer 1 minute longer then remove from the heat. Stir in the vanilla and pour into a serving bowl. Cover and cool **Serves about 5 at approximately 180 calories per serving.**

Minted Yogurt Mould

Very smooth and pleasantly tart.

6 sponge fingers
15 g/$\frac{1}{2}$ oz powdered gelatine
2 tablespoons water
225 g/8 oz sugar
4 tablespoons unsweetened cocoa powder
250 ml/8 fl oz skimmed milk
$\frac{1}{4}$ teaspoon peppermint essence
300 ml/$\frac{1}{2}$ pint natural yogurt
2 egg whites
$\frac{1}{8}$ teaspoon cream of tartar

Halve the sponge fingers lengthways, then halve each one crossways. Stand the sponge finger quarters upright, rounded end up, around the side of a 20-cm/8-in springform tin and set aside. Sprinkle the gelatine over the water; set aside to soften. In a medium-sized saucepan, stir together the sugar and cocoa. Add the skimmed milk and bring to a boil over medium-low heat, stirring constantly. Add the gelatine mixture. Boil, stirring contantly, over low heat for about 10 minutes or until the mixture reaches 105 C, 220 F on a sugar thermometer. Remove from the heat and stir in the peppermint essence; set aside to cool for 20 to 25 minutes. In a large bowl, stir the yogurt until smooth. Blend in the cooled chocolate mixture and refrigerate for 20 to 25 minutes. In a small bowl, beat the egg whites until foamy. Add the cream of tartar and continue beating until stiff but not dry. Stir a heaped tablespoon of beaten egg white into the chilled chocolate mixture, then fold the remaining egg white into the chocolate mixture until blended. Pour into the prepared tin. Refrigerate for at least 3 hours or overnight. **Serves 8, about 160 calories per serving.**

Chocolate Fondue

Get out your fondue pot and enjoy chocolate in a new way.

175 g/6 oz plain chocolate
300 ml/$\frac{1}{2}$ pint single cream
175 g/6 oz sugar
100 g/4 oz butter or margarine
generous pinch of salt
3 tablespoons crème de cacao or coffee-flavoured liqueur
sponge cake squares
whole strawberries
banana slices
orange sections

In a saucepan, melt the chocolate in the cream over very low heat. Stir in the sugar, butter or margarine and salt. Stir constantly over very low heat until smooth. Stir in the liqueur. Pour into a fondue pot and place over heat. With fondue forks or long skewers, dip cake squares or fruits into the sauce. **Makes about 750 ml/1$\frac{1}{4}$ pints.**

Mocha Fondue

100 g/4 oz butter or margarine
350 g/12 oz plain chocolate, broken into pieces
scant 150 ml/$\frac{1}{4}$ pint evaporated milk
2 tablespoons instant coffee powder
marshmallows
chunks of pound cake
banana chunks
orange sections

In a medium-sized saucepan over low heat, stirring constantly, melt the butter or margarine and chocolate pieces. Stir in the evaporated milk and coffee powder. Pour into a fondue pot and place over heat. With fondue forks or long skewers, dip marshmallows, cake or fruits into fondue. **Makes about 600 ml/1 pint.**

Pears Hélène

Decorate this easy-to-make version of the classic dessert with whipped cream.

8 tinned pear halves
25 g/1 oz plain chocolate, broken in small chunks
3 tablespoons water
50 g/2 oz sugar
75 g/3 oz golden syrup
15 g/½ oz butter or margarine
4 scoops vanilla ice cream
whipped cream, if desired
maraschino cherries, if desired

Refrigerate the pears. Combine the chocolate, water, sugar and golden syrup in a small saucepan. Stir constantly over low heat until the chocolate melts. Remove from the heat and beat in the butter or margarine. If the sauce is not smooth, beat with a wire whisk or rotary beater. Set aside to cool for about 5 minutes. Drain the chilled pears. Place a scoop of ice cream in the centre of each of the 4 pear halves. Top with the remaining pear halves, forming 4 whole stuffed pears. Spoon about 2 tablespoons chocolate sauce into each of 4 dessert dishes. Stand one whole stuffed pear on end in chocolate sauce in each dessert dish. Spoon the remaining chocolate sauce over each. If desired, pipe a ruffle of whipped cream around the edges of the pears where the halves come together. Top with a cherry, if desired. **Serves 4.**

Variation

Use 4 whole fresh pears. Peel, halve and core them. In a medium-sized saucepan, combine 475 ml/16 fl oz water and 225 g/8 oz sugar. Bring to a boil, drop in the pears and simmer until tender. Remove from the heat and refrigerate in the syrup. Proceed as directed.

Bavarian Crêpes

Indescribably elegant and delicious.

2 eggs
300 ml/½ pint buttermilk
75 g/3 oz flour
2 tablespoons sugar
2 tablespoons unsweetened cocoa powder
25 g/1 oz butter, melted
Cherry Filling (see below)
300 ml/½ pint soured cream
25 g/1 oz plain chocolate, grated
CHERRY FILLING
2 (425-g/15-oz) cans stoneless black cherries
100 g/4 oz icing sugar
2 tablespoons cornflour
100 ml/4 fl oz almond liqueur
300 ml/½ pint soured cream
25 g/1 oz plain chocolate, grated

In a medium-sized bowl, beat the eggs slightly. Add the buttermilk and beat with a whisk or an electric mixer on low speed until just blended. Add the flour, sugar and cocoa, beating with a whisk or an electric mixer on medium speed until smooth. Beat in the melted butter. Let the batter stand for about 30 minutes at room temperature. If kept longer before cooking, refrigerate. Stir the batter through with a spoon. Cook the crêpes in a crêpe or omelette pan. As each crêpe is cooked, stack in a covered dish to keep warm and moist. Finally prepare the Cherry Filling and spoon it onto the warm cooked crêpes. Fold the sides over the filling, like an envelope. Spoon the soured cream on top, sprinkle with the grated chocolate and serve immediately. **Serves 14 to 16.**

Cherry Filling

Drain the cherries, reserving 4 tablespoons of the juice. In a medium-sized saucepan, combine the icing sugar and cornflour. Stir in the liqueur and reserved cherry juice and add the drained cherries. Stir constantly over moderate heat until slightly thickened.

Soufflés and Cheesecakes

Soufflés have always had a mysterious aura about them. Actually, there are two different kinds of soufflés: both are light because stiffly beaten egg whites are folded into the batter. Cold soufflés depend on gelatine to keep them airy and should be refrigerated for several hours or overnight before serving. Hot soufflés depend on heat from the oven to make them rise, so timing is the key to their success. They must be served as soon as they are taken out of the oven.

You can either beat egg whites in a copper bowl with a wire whisk (which is best), or in a bowl with an electric beater. A chemical reaction between the copper bowl and egg whites makes them more stable, so cream of tartar is not necessary but we have included cream of tartar in our recipes in case you use a non-copper bowl.

When making a dessert soufflé, first lightly oil the soufflé dish, then sprinkle it with sugar.

A paper collar is essential to stabilise a cold soufflé as the mixture generally comes up above the top of the dish. If you don't want to use a collar, use a larger soufflé dish.

To prepare a soufflé dish with a collar, lightly oil the soufflé dish and sprinkle it with sugar. Tear off about 56 cm/22 in of foil for a 1-litre/2-pint soufflé dish or 70 cm/28 in for the 1.75-litre/3-pint size. Fold foil lengthwise in thirds to form a 56 or 70-cm/22 or 28-in × 10-cm/4-in strip. Lightly oil one side of the strip and sprinkle with sugar. Wrap around the soufflé dish with the oiled side inside, letting 3–5 cm/1½–2 in of foil extend above the top of the dish. Overlap the ends and secure with tape or string. Fill with soufflé mixture and either bake or refrigerate, depending on the kind of soufflé. At serving time, carefully remove the collar.

Cheesecakes are not difficult, but you should allow enough time to make them and to let them cool properly.

If you haven't tried a chocolate cheesecake, you will find it hard to believe why people are so enthusiastic about these irresistible desserts. But try them with chocolate in the filling, the crust, topping, or in all three; and you can add compatible flavours such as orange or mint to enhance the chocolate.

Mocha Soufflé

250 ml/8 fl oz milk
75 g/3 oz plain chocolate, broken into small pieces
5 egg yolks
100 g/4 oz sugar
2 tablespoons flour
2 tablespoons cornflour
1 tablespoon butter
1 tablespoon coffee liqueur
5 egg whites
$\frac{1}{4}$ teaspoon cream of tartar

Prepare a 1.75-litre/3-pint soufflé dish as described opposite; set aside. Set the oven at 180 C, 350 F, gas 4. In a medium-sized saucepan over low heat, combine the milk and chocolate. Stir until the chocolate melts then remove from the heat and set aside. In a medium-sized bowl, beat the egg yolks until thickened and pale yellow in colour. Beat in the sugar, flour and cornflour until smooth. Add to the melted chocolate in the saucepan and return to the heat. Stir over low heat until the mixture thickens. Remove from heat, stir in the butter and liqueur and set aside. In a large bowl, beat the egg whites until foamy. Add the cream of tartar and continue beating until stiff peaks form. Fold in the chocolate mixture, spoon into the prepared dish and bake for 45 minutes. Serve immediately. **Serves 6 to 8.**

Cocoa Soufflé

175 g/6 oz sugar
40 g/1$\frac{1}{2}$ oz unsweetened cocoa powder
3 tablespoons cornflour
175 ml/6 fl oz milk
50 g/2 oz butter or margarine
1 teaspoon vanilla essence
4 egg yolks
4 egg whites
$\frac{1}{4}$ teaspoon cream of tartar
icing sugar or sweetened whipped cream

Prepare a 1-litre/2-pint soufflé dish as described on page 00, and set it aside. Preheat the oven to 160 C, 325 F, gas 3. In a medium-sized saucepan, combine the sugar, cocoa and cornflour. Gradually stir in the milk. Stir constantly over low heat until the mixture is thickened and smooth. Remove from the heat, stir in the butter or margarine and vanilla and set aside to cool. In a medium-sized bowl, beat the egg yolks until thickened and pale yellow in colour. Stir in the cocoa mixture. In a large bowl, beat the egg whites until foamy. Add the cream of tartar and continue beating until the egg whites are stiff but not dry. Stir about one-third of the beaten egg whites into the cocoa mixture, then gently fold the cocoa mixture into the remaining egg whites. Pour into the prepared soufflé dish. Bake for about 55 minutes. Serve immediately, dusted with icing sugar or topped with sweetened whipped cream. **Serves 6 to 8.**

How to make Crème de Cacao Soufflé

1 To make a collar for a soufflé dish, lightly oil the soufflé dish and sprinkle with sugar. For a 1.75-litre/3-pint dish, fold a 70-cm/28-in long piece of foil lengthwise into thirds. Lightly oil one side of the foil and sprinkle with sugar. Wrap the foil around the outside of the dish. Secure it with tape or string.

2 Set the prepared dish aside. Cook and chill the chocolate mixture then fold the chilled mixture into stiffy beaten egg whites. Fold whipped cream into the chocolate mixture. Spoon into the prepared soufflé dish.

3 Allow plenty of time for the soufflé to set. Chill for 6 hours or overnight so it will be thoroughly chilled and firm. Then carefully remove the foil collar by removing the tape or string and slowly pulling the foil away from the chilled soufflé.

4 Just before serving, whip the cream. Put it into the piping bag fitted with a decorative nozzle. Form small mounds of cream around the edge and in the middle of the soufflé. Sprinkle with grated chocolate.

Crème de Cacao Soufflé

The cool elegance of this soufflé will make a lasting impression.

225 g/8 oz sugar
25 g/1 oz gelatine
$\frac{1}{4}$ teaspoon salt
225 ml/8 fl oz water
6 egg yolks, slightly beaten
175 g/6 oz plain chocolate, broken into pieces
3 tablespoons crème de cacao liqueur
6 egg whites
300 ml/$\frac{1}{2}$ pint whipping cream
grated chocolate or chocolate curls
whipped cream, if desired

Prepare a 900-ml/1$\frac{1}{2}$-pint soufflé dish with a collar as shown on page 80; set aside. Mix half of the sugar, the gelatine and salt in a medium-sized saucepan. Stir in the water, add the slightly beaten egg yolks and chocolate pieces. Stir constantly over medium heat until the chocolate melts and the mixture begins to simmer. Remove from the heat and stir in the crème de cacao. Chill until the mixture mounds slightly when dropped from a spoon. In a large bowl, beat the egg whites until foamy. Gradually beat in the rest of the sugar and continue beating until stiff and glossy. Fold the chilled chocolate mixture into the beaten egg whites. In a medium-sized bowl, beat the cream until stiff. Fold into the chocolate mixture. Carefully spoon into the prepared soufflé dish and refrigerate for 6 to 8 hours or until set. Just before serving, remove the foil band. Decorate with grated chocolate or chocolate curls and whipped cream, if desired. **Serves 10 to 12.**

Plantation Soufflé

A cool and refreshing way to end a meal.

3 tablespoons cold water
4 tablespoons crème de menthe
15 g/$\frac{1}{2}$ oz gelatine
150 g/5 oz soft brown sugar
175 g/6 oz plain chocolate, broken into pieces
$\frac{1}{4}$ teaspoon salt
4 egg yolks
4 egg whites
300 ml/$\frac{1}{2}$ pint whipping cream

Combine the water and crème de menthe in a medium-sized saucepan. Sprinkle with the gelatine and add half the brown sugar. Stir constantly over low heat until the gelatine and sugar dissolve. Add the chocolate pieces and salt and stir until the chocolate melts. Remove from the heat and stir in the egg yolks one at a time. Cool. In a small bowl, beat the egg whites until stiff but not dry. Gradually beat in the rest of the brown sugar and continue beating until very stiff peaks form. Fold into the chocolate gelatine mixture. Whip the cream and fold into the chocolate-gelatine mixture. Turn into a 1.75-litre/3-pint soufflé dish. Refrigerate for several hours or overnight. **Serves 6.**

Coconut Soufflé

A delightfully flavoured soufflé that holds up well.

100 g/4 oz cooking chocolate
6 egg yolks
50 g/2 oz sugar
225 g/8 oz full fat soft cream cheese, at room temperature
75 g/3 oz full fat soft cream cheese, at room temperature
whipping cream
50 g/2 oz desiccated coconut
6 egg whites
$\frac{1}{4}$ teaspoon cream of tartar

Melt the chocolate and set it aside. Prepare a 1-litre/2-pint soufflé dish as described on page 00; set aside. Set the oven at 180 C, 350 F, gas 4. In a medium-sized bowl, beat the egg yolks until thickened and pale yellow in colour. Beat in the sugar. Cut the cream cheese into small cubes, add them to the egg mixture and beat until smooth. Stir in the cream, coconut and melted chocolate. In a large bowl, beat the egg whites until foamy. Add the cream of tartar and continue beating until stiff but not dry. Stir about one-third of the beaten egg whites into the chocolate mixture, then gently fold the chocolate mixture into the remaining egg whites. Pour into the prepared soufflé dish and bake for about 55 minutes. Serve immediately. **Serves 6 to 8.**

Fudge Soufflé

A light and airy soufflé with a deep fudge flavour.

175 g/6 oz sugar
50 g/2 oz flour
300 ml/$\frac{1}{2}$ pint milk
175 g/6 oz plain chocolate
2 tablespoons crème de cacao liqueur
6 egg yolks
6 egg whites
$\frac{1}{4}$ teaspoon cream of tartar
icing sugar

Prepare a 1.75-litre/3-pint soufflé dish as described on page 80; set aside. Set the oven at 160 C, 325 F, gas 3. In a medium-sized saucepan, combine the sugar and flour. Stir in the milk. Stir constantly over low heat until thickened. Add the chocolate and stir until smooth. Remove from heat and stir in the crème de cacao. In a medium-sized bowl, beat the egg yolks until thickened and pale yellow in colour. Stir in the chocolate mixture. In a large bowl, beat the egg whites until foamy. Add the cream of tartar and beat until stiff but not dry. Fold about one-third of the beaten egg whites into the chocolate mixture, then fold the chocolate mixture into the remaining egg whites. Spoon into the prepared soufflé dish and bake for about 1 hour and 5 minutes. Sprinkle with icing sugar and serve immediately. **Serves 6 to 8.**

Elegant Cheesecake

This has to be the ultimate in cheesecakes.

CRUST
175 g/6 oz digestive biscuits, crushed
2 tablespoons sugar
75 g/3 oz butter or margarine, melted

FILLING
75 g/3 oz plain chocolate
450 g/1 lb full fat soft cream cheese, at room temperature
225 g/8 oz sugar
4 egg yolks
350 ml/12 fl oz soured cream
25 g/1 oz flour
1½ teaspoons vanilla essence
4 egg whites

First make the cheesecake base. In a medium-sized bowl, mix the biscuit crumbs, sugar and melted butter or margarine. Press on the bottom and sides of a 23-cm/9-in springform tin, then refrigerate.

Melt the chocolate and set it aside to cool. Set the oven at 180 C, 350 F, gas 4. In a large bowl, beat the cream cheese and sugar until light and creamy. Beat in the egg yolks one at a time until blended. Stir the soured cream into the cooled chocolate. Add the chocolate mixture, flour and vanilla to the egg yolk mixture. Beat until smooth. In a small bowl, beat the egg whites until stiff but not dry and fold them into the chocolate mixture. Spoon into the prepared crust and bake for 55 to 60 minutes or until the filling is firm. Turn off the oven and let the cake cool in it with the door ajar for 1 hour. Cool in the tin on a wire rack. Refrigerate for several hours before cutting. **Serves 10 to 12.**

Regal Cheesecake

Cottage cheese is the nutritious base for this tasty dessert.

BASE
175 g/6 oz gingernut biscuits, crushed
2 tablespoons sugar
75 g/3 oz butter or margarine, melted

FILLING
450 g/1 lb cottage cheese
4 egg yolks
1 teaspoon vanilla essence
¼ teaspoon almond essence
275 g/10 oz sugar
75 g/3 oz flour
½ teaspoon salt
50 g/2 oz cooking chocolate, melted
250 g/8 fl oz soured cream
4 egg whites

First make the base. In a small bowl, mix the biscuit crumbs, sugar and melted butter or margarine and set aside about 4 tablespoons of the mixture. Press the remaining crumb mixture on the bottom and about 3.5–5 cm/1½–2 in up the sides of a 23-cm/9-in springform tin; refrigerate. Set the oven at 160 C, 325 F, gas 3. In a large bowl, beat the cottage cheese until the curds are partially broken up. Beat in the egg yolks one at a time. Add the vanilla and almond essences, the sugar, flour and salt and beat until blended. Beat in the chocolate mixture and soured cream. In a small bowl, beat the egg whites until stiff but not dry and fold them into the chocolate mixture. Pour into the prepared biscuit crust and sprinkle over the reserved crumb mixture. Bake for 50 to 55 minutes then turn off oven and let the cake cool in the oven with the door ajar for 1 hour. Refrigerate for several hours in the tin then remove the side of the tin. Cut the cheesecake into wedges. **Serves 10 to 12.**

Orange-glazed Cheesecake

Silky smooth texture and incredible flavour.

BASE
150 g/5 oz chocolate digestive biscuits, crushed
2 tablespoons sugar
$\frac{1}{4}$ teaspoon cinnamon
75 g/3 oz butter or margarine, melted
FILLING
450 g/1 lb full fat soft cream cheese, at room temperature
275 g/10 oz sugar
25 g/1 oz unsweetened cocoa powder
$\frac{1}{4}$ teaspoon almond essence
2 eggs
250 ml/8 fl oz soured cream
65 g/2$\frac{1}{2}$ oz sugar
2 tablespoons cornflour
175 ml/6 fl oz orange juice
3 tablespoons orange liqueur
2 oranges, peeled and divided in segments
whipped cream, if desired

First prepare the base. In a small bowl, combine the biscuit crumbs, 2 tablespoons sugar, cinnamon and melted butter or margarine. Press on the bottom and 3.5 cm/1$\frac{1}{2}$ in up the side of a 20-cm/8-in springform tin; refrigerate.

Set the oven at 180 C, 350 F, gas 4. In a large bowl, cream the cheese, 225 g/8 oz of the sugar and the cocoa. Add the almond essence and eggs, beating until smooth. Stir in the soured cream. Pour into the prepared crust. Bake 45 to 50 minutes. Cool in the tin for several hours. In a small saucepan, combine the rest of the sugar and the cornflour. Stir in the orange juice and bring to a boil over medium heat, stirring constantly. Simmer for 1 minute, then remove the glaze from the heat and add the liqueur. Cool to lukewarm. Spoon half of the glaze over the cooled cheesecake and arrange the orange segments on top. Spoon the remaining glaze over the orange segments. Chill until firm then remove the side of the tin. Decorate with whipped cream, if desired. Cut the cheesecake into wedges. **Serves 8 to 10.**

Cocoa Cheesecake

A smooth chocolate cheesecake with a soured cream topping.

BASE
150 g/5 oz chocolate digestive biscuits, crushed
2 tablespoons sugar
75 g/3 oz butter or margarine, melted
FILLING
450 g/1 lb full fat soft cream cheese, at room temperature
275 g/10 oz sugar, plus 2 tablespoons
25 g/1 oz unsweetened cocoa powder
1 teaspoon vanilla essence
2 eggs
250 ml/8 fl oz soured cream
$\frac{1}{2}$ teaspoon vanilla essence

First, prepare the base. In a small bowl, combine the biscuit crumbs, 2 tablespoons sugar and the melted butter or margarine. Press on the bottom and 3.5 to 5 cm/1$\frac{1}{2}$ to 2 in up the side of a 20-cm/8-in springform cake tin; refrigerate. Set the oven at 180 C, 375 F, gas 4.

In a medium-sized bowl, cream the cheese, the 275 g/10 oz sugar and the cocoa. Add vanilla and eggs, beating until smooth, then pour into the prepared crust. Bake for 25 minutes. Remove from the oven but do not turn it off. In a small bowl, combine the soured cream, the remaining 2 tablespoons sugar and vanilla. Spread over the top of the baked filling, return to the oven and bake for a further 10 minutes. Cool for several hours or overnight. Remove the side of the tin and cut the cheesecake into wedges. **Serves 10 to 12.**

Orange-glazed Cheesecake

Tortes and Pies

There may be arguments about the definition of a torte, but everyone agrees that tortes are not only a delicious dessert, but also a dramatic one. To avoid confusion, we have grouped cake-type tortes with baked meringues.

If you enjoy the kind of torte that's made like a rich cake using ground nuts or crumbs for part or all of the flour, we have several of the best. If you are fond of the traditional type of torte, try our version of Sacher Torte or Caramel Torte en Croûte.

One of our favourite chocolate pies is Brownie Pie: similar to an American brownie, but made in a flan tin without a crust, it's a quick and easy dessert you can make ahead of time and serve with ice cream.

You can mix or match pie crusts and fillings. That is, fill a chocolate crust with chocolate filling, or make a standard pie crust for the base of a Grasshopper Pie or Black Bottom Pie.

When making pie fillings with chocolate, milk and eggs, use heat in moderation. Chocolate scorches easily so the mixture needs to be watched carefully and stirred frequently. In case the filling you cooked on top of the stove still has flecks of unmelted chocolate in it, beat it slightly with a wire whisk or hand mixer before pouring it into the pie shell.

Whipped cream is the crowning glory for many chocolate pies. Just before serving, whip the cream and spoon it on top of the pie. For a more elegant look, put the whipped cream into a piping bag and pipe a wide ruffle around the pie's edge or make rosettes on each slice. A sprinkle of grated chocolate makes a decorative finishing touch too.

Sacher Torte

One of the most famous tortes.

100 g/4 oz plain chocolate
175 g/6 oz butter or margarine
175 g/6 oz sugar
5 egg yolks
75 g/3 oz flour
5 egg whites
6 tablespoons apricot jam
Honey Glaze (see below)
HONEY GLAZE
100 g/4 oz plain chocolate
1 tablespoon honey
50 g/2 oz butter

Melt the chocolate and set it aside. Grease and flour a 23-cm/9-in springform tin; set aside. Set the oven at 160 C, 325 F, gas 3. In a large bowl, cream the butter or margarine and sugar until creamy. Add the egg yolks one at a time, beating until light and fluffy. Mix in the melted chocolate. Gradually beat in the flour. In a medium-sized bowl, beat the egg whites until stiff but not dry and fold them into the chocolate mixture. Spoon into the prepared tin and bake for 50 to 60 minutes. Let stand in the tin on a cooling rack for 10 minutes. Remove the outside ring of the tin and cool the cake on the rack. Sieve the apricot jam and, when the cake is cool, split it horizontally. Spread the jam on the bottom layer, replace the top layer.

Finally prepare the Honey Glaze and spoon over the top of the cooled cake, letting the excess drip down the sides. **Serves 8 to 10.**

Honey Glaze

In a small saucepan over very low heat, melt the chocolate with the honey and butter. Stir until smooth then remove from the heat. Stir over iced water until slightly thickened and syrupy.

Walnut Torte

A traditional French torte adapted to contemporary taste.

150 g/5 oz plain chocolate
175 g/6 oz walnuts
225 g/8 oz sugar
2 tablespoons flour
175 g/6 oz butter
5 egg yolks
5 egg whites
Chocolate Whipped Cream (see below)
walnut halves, if desired
CHOCOLATE WHIPPED CREAM
100 g/4 oz cooking chocolate
300 ml/$\frac{1}{2}$ pint whipping cream
$\frac{1}{2}$ teaspoon vanilla essence

Melt the chocolate and set it aside. Grease and flour a 23-cm/9-in springform tin and set aside also. Set the oven at 180 C, 350 F, gas 4. Place the walnuts, 2 tablespoons of the sugar and the flour in the blender container and blend until the walnuts are finely ground. In a large bowl, cream the butter. Add the rest of the sugar and beat until light. Add the egg yolks one at a time, beating well after each addition. Stir in the melted chocolate, then the nut mixture. In a large bowl, beat the egg whites until stiff, then fold them into the chocolate batter. Spoon into the prepared tin and bake for about 40 minutes. Cool in the tin on a wire rack for 10 minutes, then remove the side of the tin and leave to cool completely on the rack.

Prepare the Chocolate Whipped Cream and spread it on top of the cooled cake. Decorate with walnut halves, if desired. **Serves 8 to 10.**

Chocolate Whipped Cream

Melt the chocolate and cool to lukewarm. Beat the cream until stiff and stir in the vanilla. Fold the cooled chocolate into the whipped cream.

Caramel Torte en Croûte

150 g/5 oz flour
300 g/11 oz sugar
225 g/8 oz chilled butter, cut in small chunks
2 egg yolks, slightly beaten
6 tablespoons water
100 g/4 oz honey
100 ml/4 fl oz water
450 g/1 lb chopped walnuts
50 g/2 oz butter, at room temperature
225 ml/8 fl oz milk
Chocolate Glaze (see below)
CHOCOLATE GLAZE
175 g/6 oz plain chocolate, broken into pieces
2 teaspoons cooking oil
50 g/2 oz unsalted butter

Butter a baking tray. Place the outside ring of a 28-cm/11-in flan tin and set it aside. In a large bowl, combine the flour with 50 g/2 oz of the sugar. Add the 225 g/8 oz chilled butter. Beat until the mixture resembles soft fine breadcrumbs. Beat in the egg yolks with 6 tablespoons water. By hand, quickly form into a ball and wrap in greaseproof paper or foil. Refrigerate for 30 minutes. Roll two-thirds of the dough into a 30-cm/12-in circle. Refrigerate the remaining dough. Fit the rolled dough into the flan ring on the baking tray, leaving a 1-cm/½-in overhang. Refrigerate for 30 minutes. Combine the rest of the sugar, the honey and water in a medium-sized saucepan. Bring to a boil over medium heat. Cover and continue to boil for 2 minutes. Remove the cover and boil over medium heat until the mixture is a medium caramel colour. Remove from the heat and stir in all but 2 tablespoons of the chopped walnuts, the softened butter and the milk. Return to the heat, bring to a boil, then simmer over low heat for 15 minutes, stirring occasionally. Set the oven at 220 C, 425 F, gas 7. To assemble, roll the remaining dough into a 28-cm/11-in circle. Quickly pour the filling into the pastry-lined flan ring. Brush the overhanging pastry edges with water. Place the circle of pastry over the filling. Bring the overhanging pastry over the 28-cm/11-in circle and press lightly to seal. Cut a slit in the centre and bake for 20 minutes. Let cool in the ring on a baking tray for 4 hours. Invert the cooled torte onto a large serving plate and remove the flan ring. Prepare the Chocolate Glaze. Pour it over the top of the torte, letting the excess drip down the sides. Sprinkle the reserved chopped walnuts around the top edge. Chill the torte for easier cutting. Cut into wedges. **Serves 12 to 14.**

Chocolate Glaze

Melt the chocolate pieces then stir in the oil and butter.

Meringue Torte

5 egg whites
1 teaspoon vanilla essence
275 g/10 oz granulated sugar
300 ml/½ pint whipping cream
2 tablespoons icing sugar
1 tablespoon unsweetened cocoa powder
grated chocolate, if desired

Line 2 large baking trays with brown paper. Draw a 23-cm/9-in circle on each sheet of paper and set aside. Set the oven at 120 C, 250 F, gas ½. In a large bowl, beat the egg whites until soft peaks form. Add vanilla then, gradually, the granulated sugar, beating until very thick and glossy. Spoon the beaten egg whites onto each circle and spread with a spatula to fill each circle. Bake for 40 to 45 minutes or until very lightly coloured and crisp. Cool for about 10 minutes then very carefully lift meringues off the paper and leave till cool.

In a medium-sized bowl, beat the cream until it begins to thicken then gradually beat in the icing sugar and fold in the cocoa. Stack the baked meringues with cream filling between each meringue and on top. Refrigerate several hours. Decorate with grated chocolate, if desired. **Serves 10 to 12.**

How to make Caramel Torte en Croûte

1 While the pastry dough is refrigerating, place the ring of a 28-cm/11-in flan tin on a large buttered baking tray. Roll out two-thirds of the chilled dough into a 30-cm/12-in circle. Fit the circle into the bottom and over the sides of the flan ring. Allow about 1 cm/$\frac{1}{2}$ in overhang. Chill the pastry while you are making the filling.

2 Boil the sugar, honey and water until the mixture is caramel coloured. Add the walnuts, butter and milk and simmer for another 15 minutes. Spoon the filling into the cooled pastry-lined flan ring.

3 Roll the remaining chilled pastry into a 28-cm/11-in circle and place over the filling in the flan ring. Brush the overhanging pastry with water, then fold it over the 28-cm/11-in pastry circle. Gently press the edges to seal. Don't worry about neat edges because this will be the bottom of the torte. Cut a slit in the centre of the pastry and bake.

4 When the torte is baked, let it cool on the baking tray for about 4 hours, then invert it onto a large serving plate and remove the flan ring. Spread the torte with glaze and sprinkle with nuts. This torte is quite rich so you can serve it in small slices.

Dobos Torte

You'll need 6 layers, so refill your cake tin while the first layers are cooling.

450 g/1 lb softened butter
450 g/1 lb sugar
4 whole eggs and 6 egg yolks
175 g/6 oz flour
1 teaspoon vanilla essence
100 g/4 oz plain chocolate
$\frac{1}{4}$ teaspoon cream of tartar
scant 150 ml/$\frac{1}{4}$ pint water
THE GLAZE
175 g/6 oz sugar
4 tablespoons water

Grease and flour 23-cm/9-in cake tins; set aside. Set the oven at 180 C, 350 F, gas 4. In a large bowl, cream 225 g/8 oz of the butter and 225 g/8 oz of the sugar until light and fluffy. Beat in the whole eggs, then stir in the flour and vanilla until the batter is smooth. Spoon about one-sixth of the batter about 3 mm/$\frac{1}{8}$ in thick into each prepared tin. Bake for 7 to 9 minutes or until lightly browned around the edges then remove from the tin. Cool on a wire rack and repeat until all the batter is used and you have 6 cool layers. Melt the chocolate and set it aside. In a medium-sized saucepan, combine the rest of the sugar, cream of tartar and water. Stir over low heat until the sugar dissolves, then boil on a moderate heat without stirring until the syrup reaches 115 C, 283 F on a sugar thermometer, or the soft-ball stage. While the syrup is cooking, beat the egg yolks in a medium-sized bowl until thick and pale yellow in colour. Gradually pour the hot syrup over the beaten eggs, beating until the mixture is lukewarm and creamy. Beat in the rest of the butter, then the melted chocolate. Spread a thin layer of filling between the cake layers but not on the top layer.

To make the glaze, in a small heavy saucepan, combine the sugar and water and cook over moderate heat without stirring until the sugar dissolves and begins to darken, 10 to 12 minutes. Occasionally swirling the pan, continue to boil until the glaze becomes golden brown, then immediately pour it over the top cake layer. With a buttered knife, quickly mark the glaze into 12 to 16 equal-sized wedges, cutting almost but not quite through it. Refrigerate for several hours or overnight. **Serves 10 to 12.**

Orange Chocolate Torte

A meringue-like torte crunchy with biscuit crumbs and nuts.

175 g/6 oz digestive biscuits, crushed
100 g/4 oz walnuts
3 egg whites
$\frac{1}{4}$ teaspoon cream of tartar
225 g/8 oz sugar
1 teaspoon grated orange rind
75 g/3 oz plain chocolate, broken into pieces
Orange Chocolate Glaze (see below)
ORANGE CHOCOLATE GLAZE
175 g/6 oz plain chocolate, broken into pieces
150 ml/$\frac{1}{4}$ pint soured cream
2 tablespoons orange liqueur

Butter a 23-cm/9-in springform tin and set it aside. Set the oven at 180 C, 350 F, gas 4. In a blender, pulverize the digestive biscuits to fine crumbs, then set aside. Pulverize the nuts to fine crumbs also and set aside. In a medium-sized bowl, beat the egg whites and cream of tartar until foamy. Gradually add the sugar, beating until stiff and glossy. Fold in the biscuit crumbs, walnut crumbs and orange rind, then the chocolate pieces. Bake for 25 to 30 minutes. Cool in the tin then remove from it.

Prepare the Orange Chocolate Glaze. Spread on the cooled torte, letting the excess drip down the sides. Cut in wedges. **Serves 6.**

Orange Chocolate Glaze

In the top of a double boiler over hot but not boiling water, melt the chocolate pieces, stirring until smooth. Stir in the soured cream and liqueur.

Almond and Cherry Squares

50 g/2 oz blanched almonds
100 g/4 oz plain chocolate
50 g/2 oz butter or margarine
75 g/3 oz sugar
4 egg yolks
4 egg whites
$\frac{1}{8}$ teaspoon cream of tartar
100 g/4 oz dark cherries, stoned
whipped cream

Grind the almonds in a food processor or blender and set aside. Melt the chocolate and set it aside also. Grease and flour a 20-cm/8-in square baking tin. Set the oven at 180 c, 350 f, gas 4. In a medium-sized bowl, cream the butter or margarine and all but 2 tablespoons of the sugar until fluffy. Beat in the egg yolks and stir in the melted chocolate and ground almonds. In a small bowl, beat the egg whites and cream of tartar until foamy. Gradually add the reserved sugar and beat until stiff but not dry. Fold into the chocolate mixture and pour into the prepared tin. Spoon the cherries over the top and bake for 20 to 25 minutes. Cool before cutting into 5-cm/2-in squares. Top the squares with whipped cream. **Serves 16.**

Grasshopper Pie

150 g/5 oz chocolate digestive biscuits, crushed
1 tablespoon sugar
25 g/1 oz butter or margarine, melted
32 large marshmallows
100 ml/4 fl oz milk
3 tablespoons green crème de menthe liqueur
3 tablespoons white crème de cacao
300 ml/$\frac{1}{2}$ pint whipping cream
whipped cream, if desired
grated chocolate, if desired

Combine the biscuit crumbs, sugar and melted butter or margarine, and press on the bottom and side of a 23-cm/9-in flan tin. Refrigerate while making the filling. In a medium-sized saucepan, combine the marshmallows and milk. Stir constantly over low heat until the marshmallows melt. Refrigerate until thickened. Stir in the crème de menthe and crème de cacao. In a medium-sized bowl, beat the cream until stiff. Fold in the cool marshmallow mixture and pour into the prepared crust. Refrigerate until firm. If desired, decorate with whipped cream and grated chocolate. **Serves 6 to 8.**

Overleaf Grasshopper Pie

Chocolate Buttercream Pie

100 g/4 oz plain chocolate
175 g/6 oz butter
225 g/8 oz sugar
2 teaspoons vanilla essence
4 eggs
1 23-cm/9-in pastry shell, baked
whipped cream, if desired

Melt the chocolate and set it aside to cool. In a small bowl, cream the butter. Add the sugar, melted chocolate and vanilla and beat until light and fluffy. Add the eggs and beat for about 3 minutes, until the mixture is smooth and thick. Pour into the baked pie shell; chill. Decorate with whipped cream, if desired. **Serves 6 to 8.**

Chocolate Cream Pie

This is a no-fuss pie you can depend on.

225 g/8 oz sugar
25 g/1 oz cornflour
¼ teaspoon salt
350 ml/12 fl oz water
3 eggs, slightly beaten
75 g/3 oz plain chocolate, broken in chunks
25 g/1 oz butter or margarine
1 teaspoon vanilla essence
1 23-cm/9-in pastry shell, baked
150 ml/¼ pint whipping cream

In a medium-sized saucepan, mix the sugar, cornflour and salt. Pour in the water and stir until blended. Add the eggs and chocolate. Stir constantly over low heat until thickened and smooth. Remove from the heat and stir in the butter or margarine and vanilla. Pour into the pastry shell. Refrigerate for several hours or until firm. Whip the cream and spread over the pie. **Serves 6 to 8.**

Chocolate Banana Cream Pie

100 g/4 oz sugar
½ teaspoon salt
25 g/1 oz cornflour
600 ml/1 pint milk
175 g/6 oz plain chocolate, broken into pieces
1 teaspoon vanilla essence
3 egg yolks, slightly beaten
1 23-cm/9-in pastry shell, baked
2 medium bananas
150 ml/¼ pint whipping cream

In a medium-sized saucepan, stir together the sugar, salt and cornflour. Gradually stir in the milk. Add the chocolate pieces and vanilla. Bring to a boil over medium heat, stirring constantly. Continue stirring and boiling 1 minute longer. Remove from the heat. Stir a little hot mixture into the egg yolks and mix well, then add the egg yolk mixture to the remaining hot mixture in the saucepan. Stir over low heat for 5 minutes or until thickened. Pour half the mixture into the baked pie shell. Peel the bananas and slice them crossways and layer the slices over the filling in the pie shell; cover with the remaining filling, spreading evenly. Place waxed paper directly on to the surface of the filling. Refrigerate until set, 3 to 4 hours. Before serving, whip the cream and use to decorate the edge of the pie. **Serves 6 to 8.**

Toffee Coffee Pie

225 g/8 oz shortcrust pastry mix
50 g/2 oz soft brown sugar
75 g/3 oz chopped walnuts
50 g/2 oz plain chocolate
1 teaspoon vanilla essence
1 tablespoon water
100 g/4 oz butter, softened
175 g/6 oz granulated sugar
2 teaspoons instant coffee powder
2 eggs
Coffee Cream Topping (see below)
COFFEE CREAM TOPPING
300 ml/½ pint whipping cream
2 teaspoons instant coffee powder
1 tablespoon icing sugar

Butter a 20-cm/8-in flan tin. Set the oven at 190 C, 375 F, gas 5. In a medium-sized bowl, crumble the pastry mix with a pastry blender or fork until very fine. Blend in the brown sugar, walnuts and grate in half the chocolate. Sprinkle 1 tablespoon of the mixture in a shallow baking tin and set aside. Add the vanilla and water to the remaining mixture and mix well. Press firmly into the bottom and side of the prepared tin. Moisten your fingers with cold water for easier handling. Bake for 15 minutes. Also bake the reserved tablespoon of pastry crumbs in the baking tin for 5 minutes. Cool the crust and crumbs. Melt the rest of the chocolate and set it aside to cool. In a medium-sized bowl, cream the butter then add the granulated sugar gradually, beating until light and fluffy. Stir in the cooled chocolate and instant coffee powder. Add the eggs one at a time, beating for 5 minutes after each addition. Pour into the cooled crust.

Prepare the Coffee Cream Topping and spread on top of the filling. Sprinkle with the reserved baked crumbs. Refrigerate for 2 hours before serving. **Serves 6 to 8.**

Coffee Cream Topping

In a small bowl, beat the cream until it begins to thicken. Gradually add the instant coffee powder and icing sugar, beating until stiff.

Fudge Meringue Pie

Enjoy the delicious fudge-like filling.

PIE BASE
225 g/8 oz sugar
25 g/1 oz flour
¼ teaspoon salt
milk
50 g/2 oz plain chocolate, broken in small chunks
3 egg yolks, slightly beaten
25 g/1 oz butter or margarine
1 teaspoon vanilla essence
1 23-cm/9-in pastry shell, baked and cooled
MERINGUE TOPPING
3 egg whites
½ teaspoon vanilla essence
¼ teaspoon cream of tartar
75 g/3 oz sugar

In a medium-sized saucepan, combine the sugar, flour and salt and gradually stir in the milk. Add the chocolate. Stir constantly over medium heat until bubbly. Simmer for 2 minutes longer then remove from the heat. Stir a small amount of hot mixture into the beaten egg yolks, then immediately add the egg yolk mixture to the remaining hot mixture in the saucepan. Stir constantly over a medium heat for 2 minutes then remove from the heat, add the butter or margarine and 1 teaspoon of vanilla. Pour into the cooled baked pastry shell. Set the oven at 180 C, 350 F, gas 4.

Next make the meringue. In a small bowl, beat the egg whites, vanilla essence and cream of tartar until foamy. Gradually beat in the sugar, beating until stiff and glossy. Spoon the meringue onto the chocolate filling, carefully spreading it to the edge of pie crust. Bake for 12 to 15 minutes or until golden. Cool. **Serves 6 to 8.**

Soured Cream Meringue Pie

225 g/8 oz soft brown sugar
2 tablespoons flour
¼ teaspoon cinnamon
150 ml/¼ pint soured cream
3 egg yolks, slightly beaten
25 g/1 oz butter or margarine, melted
1 teaspoon vanilla essence
175 g/6 oz plain chocolate drops
1 23-cm/9-in pastry shell, unbaked
3 egg whites
¼ teaspoon cream of tartar
50 g/2 oz granulated sugar

Set the oven at 190 C, 375 F, gas 5. In a large bowl, combine the brown sugar, flour, cinnamon, soured cream, egg yolks, melted butter or margarine and vanilla. Beat until smooth. Stir in the chocolate drops and mix well. Pour into the unbaked pastry shell. Bake for 45 to 50 minutes or until the tip of a knife inserted in the centre comes out clean. In a medium-sized bowl, beat the egg whites and cream of tartar until foamy. Gradually add the granulated sugar. Continue beating until stiff peaks form. Spread the meringue over the warm pie filling, carefully sealing to the edge of the crust. Bake for 7 to 10 minutes or until golden. Cool on a wire rack for 1 hour or so, but serve while still slightly warm. **Serves 6 to 8.**

Pecan Pie

Chocolate adds a distinctive flavour to this traditional American pie. If you cannot find pecans, walnuts make an excellent alternative.

1 23-cm/9-in pastry shell, unbaked
450 g/1 lb golden syrup
100 g/4 oz sugar
100 g/4 oz cooking chocolate
100 ml/4 fl oz evaporated milk
3 eggs, slightly beaten
100 g/4 oz pecan halves

Crimp the edge of the pastry shell so that it stands high and will hold the entire amount of filling; set aside. Set the oven at 180 C, 350 F, gas 4. In a medium-sized saucepan, combine the golden syrup, sugar, chocolate and evaporated milk. Stir constantly over low heat until the chocolate just melts. Very gradually stir the hot mixture into the beaten eggs, then stir in the pecans. Pour into the unbaked pastry shell. Bake for 50 to 60 minutes or until fairly firm. The centre will be slightly soft but become firmer as the pie cools. **Serves 6 to 8.**

Black Bottom Pie

Light and airy on top with rich chocolate underneath.

1 tablespoon powdered gelatine
3 tablespoons water
1 tablespoon cornflour
175 g/6 oz sugar
350 ml/12 fl oz milk
3 egg yolks, slightly beaten
25 g/1 oz plain chocolate, melted
1 teaspoon vanilla essence
1 23-cm/9-in pastry shell, baked
1 tablespoon rum
3 egg whites
whipped cream, if desired
grated chocolate, if desired

Sprinkle the gelatine over the water, stir and set aside. In a medium-sized saucepan, combine the cornflour and 100 g/4 oz of the sugar. Stir in the milk and cook over low heat until the mixture is slightly thickened and translucent. Remove from the heat. Stir about half of the milk mixture into the beaten egg yolks, then add the egg yolk mixture to the remaining milk mixture in the saucepan. Cook over low heat 1 minute longer.

Remove from the heat and stir in the softened gelatine. Pour about half of the hot mixture into a small bowl. Add the chocolate and vanilla and stir until blended. Pour into the baked pastry shell. Stir the rum into the remaining gelatine mixture. In a small bowl, beat the egg whites until foamy then gradually add the rest of the sugar and beat until stiff peaks form. Fold into the rum mixture. Pour over the chocolate layer in the pastry shell. Refrigerate until set. If desired, decorate with whipped cream and grated chocolate. **Serves 6 to 8.**

How to make Black Bottom Pie

1 As the name indicates, this pie has a dark chocolate bottom and light top. To make this combination, add melted chocolate to half the filling, then pour it into the bottom of the baked pie shell.

2 To make the light filling, add flavouring and sweetened stiffly beaten egg whites to the remaining filling. Then spread over the chocolate layer.

Chocolate Chiffon Pie

Rich with chocolate, yet very light.

PIE BASE
15 g/½ oz gelatine
100 g/4 oz sugar
½ teaspoon salt
300 ml/½ pint milk
75 g/3 oz plain chocolate, broken in chunks
3 egg yolks
1 teaspoon vanilla essence
MERINGUE TOPPING
3 egg whites
¼ teaspoon cream of tartar
100 g/4 oz sugar
1 23-cm/9-in pastry shell, baked
whipped cream, if desired

First, prepare the pie. In a medium-sized saucepan, combine the gelatine, sugar and salt. Gradually stir in milk. Add chocolate. Place over low heat until chocolate melts. Remove from the heat. In a small bowl, beat the egg yolks slightly. Stir a small amount of chocolate mixture into the egg yolks, then add the egg yolk mixture to the remaining chocolate mixture in the saucepan. Stir constantly until thickened. Stir in the vanilla. Cool until the mixture holds its shape when dropped from a spoon.

Next make the meringue. In a medium-sized bowl, beat the egg whites and cream of tartar until foamy. Gradually add the sugar. Beat until stiff but not dry. Fold into the cooled chocolate mixture and pour into the baked pie shell. Refrigerate for several hours. Top with whipped cream, if desired. **Serves 6 to 8.**

Peanut Crunch Pie

225 g/8 oz ground peanuts
50 g/2 oz sugar
25 g/1 oz softened butter or margarine
16 large marshmallows
50 ml/¼ pint milk
225 g/8 oz milk chocolate
300 ml/½ pint whipping cream

Set the oven at 200 C, 400 F, gas 6. In a small bowl, thoroughly combine the peanuts, sugar and butter or margarine. Press the mixture firmly and evenly against the bottom and side of a 23-cm/9-in flan tin. Bake for 6 to 8 minutes then cool. In a medium-sized saucepan, combine the marshmallows, milk and chocolate. Stir constantly over a low heat until the chocolate and marshmallows are melted and the mixture is smooth. Refrigerate, stirring occasionally, until the mixture mounds slightly when dropped from a spoon. In a small bowl, beat the whipping cream until stiff. Fold into the chocolate mixture and pour into the cooled prepared pastry shell. Refrigerate until set, about 8 hours. **Serves 6 to 8.**

Brownie Pie

2 eggs, well beaten
100 g/4 oz sugar
100 g/4 oz butter, melted
50 g/2 oz flour
40 g/1½ oz unsweetened cocoa powder
¼ teaspoon salt
1 teaspoon vanilla essence
100 g/4 oz chopped walnuts
ice cream or whipped cream, if desired

Lightly grease a 20-cm/8-in flan tin; set aside. Set the oven at 180 C, 350 F, gas 4. In a medium-sized bowl, mix the eggs with the sugar and melted butter. Stir together the flour, cocoa and salt. Add to the egg mixture. Stir in the vanilla and nuts. Pour into the prepared flan tin without a pastry shell. Bake for 20 to 25 minutes. Cool before cutting into wedges. Serve plain, with ice cream or whipped cream. **Serves 6.**

Pie Crusts

Nutty Pie Crust

100 g/4 oz walnuts or almonds
50 g/2 oz plain chocolate
25 g/1 oz butter or margarine
2 tablespoons milk
75 g/3 oz sifted icing sugar

Place the nuts in the blender container and blend until finely chopped; set aside. Lightly grease a 23-cm/9-in flan tin; set aside. In a medium-sized saucepan, combine the chocolate, butter or margarine and milk. Stir constantly over low heat until the chocolate melts. Remove from the heat and stir in the icing sugar and chopped nuts. Press on the bottom and sides of the prepared flan tin. Refrigerate until set. **Serves 6 to 8.**

Coconut Nests

A different kind of crust for a pudding, ice cream or pie filling.

100 g/4 oz cooking chocolate, broken into chunks
25 g/1 oz butter or margarine
175 g/6 oz desiccated coconut

Draw five 7.5-cm/3-in circles on waxed paper. Place on a baking tray; set aside. Place the chocolate and butter or margarine in a small saucepan. Stir constantly over low heat until the chocolate melts then remove from the heat. Stir in the coconut. Divide the coconut mixture among the circles and spread to cover each one. With the back of a small spoon, scoop out the centre and build up the sides to form nests. Refrigerate until firm. **Makes 5 nests.**

Cocoa Pie Crust

150 g/5 oz flour
65 g/2½ oz sugar
25 g/1 oz unsweetened cocoa powder
½ teaspoon salt
100 g/4 oz lard
½ teaspoon vanilla essence
2 to 3 tablespoons cold water

Set the oven at 200 C, 400 F, gas 6. In a medium-sized bowl, combine the flour, sugar, cocoa and salt. Cut in the lard with a pastry blender or 2 knives until the pieces are the size of small peas. Pour in the vanilla and cold water. Mix until the dough holds together. On a lightly floured board, roll it out 3 mm/⅛ in thick. Place in a 23-cm/9-in flan tin, trim and crimp the edges. Bake for 8 minutes. The pastry crust will be soft and bubbly but will become firmer as it cools. **Serves 6 to 8.**

Breads and Patisserie

We all take great pride in preparing freshly baked treats for our family and friends, and the fragrance of home-baked chocolate bread is the most enticing of all.

Muffins are probably the fastest and easiest bread for a spur-of-the-moment baking session: try basic Cocoa Muffins, Cinnamon Muffins or the exciting Banana-chip Muffins with a delicate chocolate flavour. Make them in muffin rings: either grease them and spoon the batter directly in, or line the muffin rings with fluted paper baking cases and pour the batter into them.

Our favourite in this section is Soured Cream Coffee Bread. It has a rich cake-like appearance with a cocoa-cinnamon mixture swirled through the middle and over the top. Serve it warm on special occasions such as Christmas morning. It can be made ahead and frozen, then thawed and warmed just before serving. If you make Soured Cream Coffee Bread for the holidays, decorate it with cherries and chocolate leaves (page 14) then lightly sift icing sugar over the top for a snowy effect.

More time consuming, but just as rewarding, are the chocolate-flavoured yeast breads. Start them 2 or 3 hours before you plan to serve them, or make them a day ahead and reheat them just before serving.

For a special treat, try Cinnamon Waffles with butter and honey for a true American brunch—or topped with ice cream for dessert.

No one can resist meringues, éclairs and cream puffs. They've always been among the most admired desserts in patisseries and on dessert trolleys in elegant restaurants. As a variation of the puff family, you'll enjoy our classic Profiteroles with chocolate saùce. They are miniature cream puffs filled with ice cream or cream and topped with chocolate. Look for other ideas for fillings for cream puffs and éclairs in the chapter on icings, fillings and sauces, pages 32 to 40.

Left to right Cinnamon Muffins and Banana Chip Muffins (overleaf)

Cocoa Muffins

1 egg
scant 150 ml/$\frac{1}{4}$ pint milk
4 tablespoons cooking oil
175 g/6 oz plain flour
100 g/4 oz sugar
3 tablespoons unsweetened cocoa powder
2 teaspoons baking powder
$\frac{1}{4}$ teaspoon salt

Grease 12 muffin rings and set them aside. Set the oven at 200 C, 400 F, gas 6. In a medium-sized bowl, beat the egg then stir in the milk and oil. Add the flour, sugar, cocoa, baking powder and salt and stir until the flour is just moistened (the batter will be slightly lumpy). Fill the prepared muffin rings two-thirds full. Bake for 20 to 25 minutes. **Makes 12 muffins.**

Banana Chip Muffins

Illustrated on page 102

175 g/6 oz flour
100 g/4 oz sugar
2 teaspoons baking powder
$\frac{1}{2}$ teaspoon salt
1 egg, slightly beaten
scant 150 ml/$\frac{1}{4}$ pint milk
3 tablespoons cooking oil
175 g/6 oz mashed ripe banana (about 2)
75 g/3 oz chocolate drops
50 g/2 oz chopped walnuts

Grease 16 muffin rings and set them aside. Set the oven at 200 C, 400 F, gas 6. In a large bowl, combine the flour, sugar, baking powder and salt. Add the egg, milk, oil and banana flesh and stir until just combined. Stir in the chocolate drops and walnuts. Spoon into the prepared muffin rings, filling each two-thirds full. Bake for 20 to 25 minutes. Serve warm. **Makes 16 muffins.**

Cinnamon Muffins

Illustrated on page 102

225 g/8 oz flour
4 teaspoons baking powder
$\frac{1}{2}$ teaspoon salt
75 g/3 oz sugar
2 eggs, slightly beaten
scant 300 ml/$\frac{1}{2}$ pint milk
50 g/2 oz butter, melted
$\frac{1}{2}$ teaspoon cinnamon
1 tablespoon cocoa powder

Grease 12 muffin rings and set them aside. Set the oven at 220 C, 425 F, gas 7. In a medium-sized bowl, combine the flour, baking powder, salt and 2 tablespoons of the sugar. In a small bowl, mix the eggs, milk and melted butter. Stir the egg mixture into the flour mixture. Combine the rest of the sugar, the cinnamon and cocoa powder. Spoon half the batter into prepared muffin rings. Sprinkle half the cinnamon-cocoa mixture over the batter in the rings, and spoon the remaining batter on top. Sprinkle with the rest of the cinnamon-cocoa mixture. Bake for 15 to 20 minutes or until golden brown. Serve hot. **Makes 12 muffins.**

Soured Cream Coffee Bread

50 g/2 oz chopped nuts
1 teaspoon cinnamon
sugar
1 tablespoon unsweetened cocoa powder
175 g/6 oz butter or margarine, softened
350 g/12 oz sugar
2 eggs
1 teaspoon vanilla essence
250 g/9 oz plain flour
2 teaspoons baking powder
$\frac{1}{2}$ teaspoon bicarbonate of soda
$\frac{1}{2}$ teaspoon salt
250 ml/8 fl oz soured cream

Grease and flour a 25-cm/10-in tin and set it aside. Set the oven at 180 C, 350 F, gas 4. In a small bowl, combine the nuts, cinnamon, 2 tablespoons of the sugar and the cocoa; set aside. In a large bowl, cream the butter or margarine and the rest of the sugar. Add the eggs and vanilla, beating until light and fluffy. Combine the flour, baking powder, bicarbonate of soda and salt. Add the flour mixture to the creamed mixture in three portions, alternating with the soured cream; beat well after each addition. Spread half of the batter in the prepared tin. Sprinkle with half the cinnamon-nut mixture then spoon in the rest of the batter and sprinkle with the remaining cinnamon-nut mixture. Bake for 45 to 50 minutes. Cool in the tin for 15 minutes. Remove from the tin and serve warm or cool. **Makes one 25-cm/10-in cake.**

Spicy Chocolate Loaf

50 g/2 oz plain chocolate
175 g/6 oz flour
225 g/8 oz sugar
1 teaspoon bicarbonate of soda
$\frac{1}{4}$ teaspoon baking powder
$\frac{1}{2}$ teaspoon salt
75 g/3 oz lard
2 eggs
$\frac{1}{4}$ teaspoon nutmeg
$\frac{1}{2}$ teaspoon cinnamon
50 g/2 oz chopped nuts

Melt the chocolate and set it aside. Grease and flour a 23 × 13-cm/9 × 5-in loaf tin and set aside also. Set the oven at 180 C, 350 F, gas 4. In a large bowl, combine all the ingredients except the chocolate and nuts. Beat for 3 minutes with an electric mixer on medium speed. Stir in the melted chocolate and nuts. Pour into the prepared tin and bake for 50 to 55 minutes. Remove from the tin and cool thoroughly before slicing. **Makes 1 loaf.**

Festive Holiday Bread

scant 300 ml/½ pint orange juice
scant 300 ml/½ pint milk
3 tablespoons cooking oil
500 g/18 oz plain flour
100 g/4 oz sugar
1 tablespoon salt
25 g/1 oz dried yeast
1 egg
175 g/6 oz plain chocolate drops
175 g/6 oz chopped crystallised fruits
1 teaspoon grated orange rind
about 275 g/10 oz flour
citrus Glaze (see below)
CITRUS GLAZE
100 g/4 oz icing sugar
15 g/½ oz butter or margarine, melted
2 tablespoons orange juice

In a small saucepan, heat the orange juice, milk and oil until very warm (50 to 55 C/120 to 130 F). In a large bowl, combine 225 g/8 oz of the flour, the sugar, salt and yeast. Add the warm milk mixture and egg. Beat at low speed until moistened, then at medium speed for 3 minutes. Stir in the chocolate drops, crystallised fruits, orange peel and enough flour to form a stiff dough. Cover and leave to rise in a warm place until doubled in bulk, 45 to 60 minutes. Generously grease a 25-cm/10-in cake tin and set aside. Set the oven at 180 C, 350 F, gas 4. Knock down the dough and spoon into the prepared tin. Bake for 40 to 50 minutes or until golden brown. Immediately remove from the tin and cool slightly. Prepare the Citrus Glaze and spoon it over the bread, letting the excess drip down the sides. **Makes one 25-cm/10-in loaf.**

Citrus Glaze

Put all the ingredients into a bowl and mix well.

Meringue Mushrooms

For best results, make these on a dry day. Use to decorate desserts or fill a pretty centrepiece basket.

3 egg whites
¼ teaspoon cream of tartar
175 g/6 oz sugar
75 g/3 oz plain or milk chocolate, broken into pieces
unsweetened cocoa powder

Line a baking tray with greaseproof paper and set it aside. Set the oven at 110 C, 225 F, gas ¼. In a small bowl, beat the egg whites until foamy. Add the cream of tartar and beat until soft peaks form. Add the sugar gradually, beating until very stiff peaks form. Place the meringue in a piping bag with a large plain nozzle 1 cm/½ in in diameter.

To make the caps: on a prepared baking tray, pipe out small mounds of meringue 2.5–3-cm/1–1½ in in diameter. Smooth the tops with a spatula. To make stems: holding the piping bag vertically and placing stems about 2.5 cm/1 in from the caps, pipe out the stems 3 cm/1½ in long. Bake for 1 to 1¼ hours or until thoroughly dry. Cool. Remove from pan.

To assemble the mushrooms: melt the chocolate pieces. With a small knife, cut a hole in the bottom of each cap to fit the stem into, and spread a layer of chocolate over the bottom of the cap. Place one end of the stem on the chocolate in the hole and leave upside down or on its side on a wire rack or in an empty egg carton until the chocolate hardens. Repeat with the remaining caps and stems. If desired, refrigerate for a few minutes but do not freeze. Sift cocoa over mushrooms to resemble real mushrooms. Cover and store at room temperature. **Makes about 20 mushrooms.**

How to make Meringue Mushrooms

1 Mushrooms and stems are made separately and then put together after they are baked. To make caps, place the meringue mixture in a piping bag with a large plain nozzle. Push out 2.5–3-cm/1–1½-in mounds of meringue onto the lined baking tray. Cut off any peaks, or smooth the tops, with a small spatula.

2 To make stems, place the meringue mixture in the piping bag with a large plain nozzle. On the lined baking tray push out stems about 3-cm/1½-in long and about 2-cm/¾-in wide. Smooth any peaks with a small spatula. Make an equal number of stems and caps.

3 Bake caps and stems until thoroughly dry. When completely cooled, put together. Hold one cap upside down and cut a small hole out of the centre. This hole is for the stem. Then spread a layer of melted chocolate into the hole and over half the bottom of the cap. Immediately place one end of the stem into the chocolate-coated hole. Stand the mushrooms on a rack until the chocolate hardens.

4 If the chocolate holding the mushrooms together does not harden at room temperature, refrigerate the mushrooms for a few minutes. When the chocolate is firm place a small amount of unsweetened cocoa powder in a small strainer or sifter. Lightly sift cocoa over the mushrooms to give them a realistic look. Use to decorate cakes or as a centrepiece.

Frosted Chocolate Doughnuts

A tantalising double-chocolate flavour.

1 egg
100 g/4 oz sugar
25 g/1 oz plain chocolate
15 g/½ oz butter or margarine
100 g/4 oz mashed potatoes
175 g/6 oz flour
3 teaspoons baking powder
½ teaspoon salt
75 ml/2½ fl oz milk
oil for frying
Chocolate Frosting (see below)
CHOCOLATE FROSTING
25 g/1 oz butter or margarine
25 g/1 oz plain chocolate
100 g/4 oz icing sugar
2 tablespoons boiling water
¼ teaspoon vanilla essence

In a large bowl, beat the egg until light, then beat in the sugar. Melt the chocolate and butter or margarine together. Add to the egg mixture. Stir in the potatoes. Combine the flour, baking powder and salt. Add milk alternately with the flour mixture. Refrigerate 1 hour. Preheat the oil or lard in a deep-fryer according to the manufacturer's directions. On a lightly floured surface, roll out the dough just under 1 cm/½ in thick. Cut with a floured doughnut cutter. Fry in hot oil for about 2 minutes or until crusty brown. Drain and cool. Prepare the Chocolate Frosting and spread on the doughnuts. **Makes 12 to 14 doughnuts.**

Chocolate Frosting

In a medium-sized saucepan, melt the butter or margarine and chocolate. Beat in the icing sugar, boiling water and vanilla. Mix well.

Éclairs

100 g/4 oz butter or margarine
225 ml/8 fl oz water
100 g/4 oz flour
¼ teaspoon salt
4 eggs
Custard Cream Filling (page 40)
Traditional Glaze (see below)
TRADITIONAL GLAZE
25 g/1 oz plain chocolate
1 teaspoon butter
100 g/4 oz sifted icing sugar
2 tablespoons hot water

Lightly grease a baking tray and set it aside. Set the oven at 200 C, 400 F, gas 6. In a medium-sized saucepan, heat the butter or margarine and water to a rolling boil. Add the flour and salt all at once and stir vigorously over low heat for about 1 minute or until the mixture becomes smooth and does not cling to the side of pan. Remove from the heat and beat in the eggs one at a time. Beat until the mixture no longer looks slippery. Assemble a piping bag with a plain round nozzle that has a 1–2-cm/½–¾-in opening. Put the mixture through the piping bag onto the prepared baking tray, forming strips 3.5 cm/1½ in thick and 11 cm/4½ in long–or use a small spoon to form strips of dough. Bake for 30 to 40 minutes. Cool away from any draught. Split the cold éclairs and fill each one with 3 to 4 tablespoons Custard Cream Filling.

Finally prepare the Traditional Glaze. Spoon over the filled éclairs, letting the excess drip down the sides. Refrigerate until serving time. **Makes 10 éclairs.**

Traditional Glaze

In a small saucepan, melt the chocolate and butter over low heat. Remove from the heat and stir in the icing sugar and water. Beat until smooth.

Cream Puffs

Even the cream puff shells are chocolate flavoured.

75 g/3 oz plain flour
1 tablespoon unsweetened cocoa powder
1 tablespoon sugar
generous pinch of salt
250 ml/8 fl oz water
100 g/4 oz butter or margarine
4 eggs
Custard Cream Filling (page 40)
Almond Butter Glaze (see below)
ALMOND BUTTER GLAZE
50 g/2 oz plain chocolate
50 g/2 oz butter or margarine
175 g/6 oz sifted icing sugar
1 tablespoon almond-flavoured liqueur
2 tablespoons hot water

Grease a baking tray and set it aside. Set the oven at 200 C, 400 F, gas 6. Stir together the flour, cocoa, sugar and salt; set aside. In a medium-sized saucepan, bring the water and butter or margarine to a boil. Quickly stir in flour mixture over low heat, beating vigorously with a spoon until the mixture forms a ball. Remove from the heat and add the eggs one at a time, beating with a spoon after each addition until the mixture is shiny and smooth. To make 9 puffs, spoon about 3 tablespoons of the mixture for each puff onto the prepared baking tray about 8 cm/3 in apart. Bake for 35 to 45 minutes or until puffed and firm. Split in half while hot then cool. Fill each cooled puff with about 3 tablespoons Custard Cream Filling. Finally prepare the Almond Glaze and immediately spoon it over the filled cream puffs, letting the excess drip down the sides. Refrigerate until serving time. **Makes 9 cream puffs.**

Almond Butter Glaze

In a small saucepan, melt the chocolate and butter or margarine over low heat. Remove from the heat. Stir in the icing sugar, liqueur and hot water. Continue stirring until smooth.

Profiteroles

Miniature cream puffs filled with ice cream and topped with rich dark chocolate.

50 g/2 oz butter or margarine
100 ml/4 fl oz water
50 g/2 oz flour
generous pinch of salt
2 eggs
Dark Chocolate Sauce (see below)
600 ml/1 pint vanilla or chocolate ice cream
DARK CHOCOLATE SAUCE
50 g/2 oz plain chocolate, broken into small chunks
3 tablespoons water
50 g/4 oz sugar
40 g/1½ oz butter or margarine
½ teaspoon vanilla essence

Lightly grease 2 baking trays and set them aside. Set the oven at 200 C, 400 F, gas 6. In a medium-sized saucepan, heat the butter or margarine and water to a rolling boil. Add flour and salt all at once. Stir vigorously over low heat for about 1 minute or until the mixture becomes smooth and does not cling to the side of the pan. Remove from the heat. Beat in the eggs one at a time and beat until the mixture no longer looks slippery. Drop from a teaspoon onto the prepared baking trays forming 33 to 36 mounds about 2 cm/¾ in across. Bake for 10 to 15 minutes. Cool away from any draughts. Prepare the Dark Chocolate Sauce. When the puffs are cool, split in half and place about 1 tablespoon ice cream inside each. Arrange in groups of 3 on individual dessert dishes. Drizzle the tops with warm chocolate sauce. Serve immediately. **Serves 11 to 12.**

Dark Chocolate Sauce

In a small saucepan over low heat, combine the chocolate, water and sugar, stirring constantly, until the chocolate melts. Bring to a boil then simmer for 5 minutes or until slightly thickened. Remove from the heat and stir in the butter or margarine and vanilla. Let cool slightly.

Cinnamon Waffles

An impressive and tasty dessert that is also very easy to make.

2 egg yolks
50 g/2 oz butter or margarine, melted
scant 300 ml/½ pint soured cream
scant 300 ml/½ pint buttermilk
100 g/4 oz flour
50 g/2 oz sugar
1 teaspoon bicarbonate of soda
¼ teaspoon salt
½ teaspoon cinnamon
2 tablespoons unsweetened cocoa powder
2 egg whites
icing sugar
1 (397-g/14-oz) can cherry or apple pie filling

In a large bowl, beat the egg yolks until thickened and pale yellow in colour. Add the melted butter or margarine, soured cream and buttermilk and beat until blended. Add the flour, sugar, bicarbonate of soda, salt, cinnamon and cocoa. Beat until smooth. Preheat the waffle iron. In a small bowl, beat the egg whites until stiff but not dry. Fold into the cocoa batter and spoon onto the preheated waffle iron. Close the lid and bake until brown and crisp. Remove from the waffle iron. Repeat until all the batter is used. Sprinkle the waffles with icing sugar and top with the pie filling. **Makes 8 or 9 waffles.**

Brownie Waffles

175 g/6 oz plain chocolate, broken into pieces
175 ml/6 fl oz milk
100 g/4 oz butter or margarine
2 egg yolks
50 g/2 oz sugar
175 g/6 oz plain flour
½ teaspoon baking powder
¼ teaspoon salt
25 g/1 oz chopped nuts
2 egg whites
ice cream

In a small saucepan over low heat, heat the chocolate pieces, milk and butter or margarine until the chocolate pieces melt. Remove from the heat and set aside. Preheat the waffle iron. In a large bowl, beat the egg yolks until thickened and pale yellow in colour. Gradually beat in the sugar then add the melted chocolate mixture, the flour, baking powder and salt. Mix well and stir in the nuts. In a small bowl, beat the egg whites until stiff but not dry and fold them into the chocolate batter. Spoon onto the preheated waffle iron, close the lid and bake until crisp. Remove from the waffle iron. Repeat until all the batter is used. Top with your favourite ice cream. **Makes about 6 waffles.**

Chantilly Lace Cones

Be prepared–have a few scraps of foil ready to prevent collapsed cones.

50 g/2 oz butter
75 g/3 oz golden syrup
40 g/1½ oz soft brown sugar
2 teaspoons unsweetened cocoa powder
generous pinch of cinnamon
50 g/2 oz flour
25 g/1 oz finely chopped nuts
450 ml/¾ pint whipping cream
3 tablespoons icing sugar
grated chocolate

Lightly grease a baking tray and set it aside. Set the oven at 190 C, 375 F, gas 5. In a medium-sized saucepan, bring the butter, golden syrup and brown sugar to a boil, stirring contantly. In a small bowl, combine the cocoa, cinnamon, flour and nuts. Gradually stir into the hot butter mixture. Drop by level tablespoonsful about 8 cm/3 in apart on to the prepared baking tray. Bake for 5 to 6 minutes then cool about 2 minutes. While still hot, turn the biscuits over with a spatula, carefully rolling each one into a cone shape. If the cones collapse, stuff them with small pieces of crumpled foil until cooled. Place seam-side down on a wire rack. If the biscuits are too firm to roll, return to the oven long enough to soften. At serving time, whip the cream until it begins to thicken. Add the icing sugar and continue beating until stiff. Spoon about 2 tablespoons whipped cream into each one. Sprinkle with grated chocolate. **Makes 12 to 14 cones.**

How to make Chantilly Lace Cones

1 These delicate biscuits should be removed from the baking trays about 2 minutes after coming out of the oven. Gently lift each one off with a spatula. Turn the biscuits over so the rough but more attractive surface will be on the outside.

2 While the biscuits are still hot, carefully roll them into cone shapes. If they collapse, stuff crumpled foil into the centres to hold them until they are set. Cool on wire racks. When cooled, remove the foil. At serving time, fill with whipped cream or ice cream.

Frozen Desserts

Chocolate-flavoured frozen desserts have always been popular. In most cases they are easy to make and contain ingredients that are readily available. A great advantage of homemade frozen desserts is the fact that you can ensure the freshness and purity of the ingredients. You can eliminate chemical emulsifiers, stabilisers and artificial flavours found in most commerical products.

Another advantage of frozen desserts is that they can be made ahead, stored in the freezer and enjoyed at any time. If you plan to store a dessert for an extended period of time, it should be tightly sealed to prevent icing and loss of moisture.

Chocolate Ice Cream

Make this classic ice cream in your ice cream machine or ice trays.

600 ml/1 pint single cream
225 g/8 oz sugar
175 g/6 oz plain chocolate, broken into pieces
3 egg yolks, slightly beaten
2 teaspoons vanilla essence
300 ml/½ pint whipping cream
3 egg whites

In a medium-sized saucepan, combine the single cream, 100 g/4 oz of the sugar and the chocolate pieces. Stir constantly over low heat until the chocolate melts. Remove from the heat and stir about half the chocolate mixture into the beaten egg yolks. Add the egg yolk mixture to the remaining chocolate mixture in the saucepan. Cook for 2 or 3 minutes or until the mixture begins to simmer. Remove from the heat and leave to cool. Stir in the vanilla and whipping cream. In a medium-sized bowl, beat the egg whites until foamy. Gradually add the rest of the sugar and continue beating until stiff. Fold the cooled chocolate mixture into the egg white mixture. Pour into an ice cream machine or shallow ice trays and freeze. **Makes 2.25 litres/4 pints.**

Milk Chocolate Ice Cream

A smooth and creamy chocolate ice cream.

225 g/8 oz sugar
1 tablespoon cornflour
750 ml/1¼ pints milk
3 egg yolks, slightly beaten
1 teaspoon vanilla essence
175 g/6 oz milk chocolate, broken into pieces
3 egg whites
300 ml/½ pint whipping cream

In a medium-sized saucepan, combine the sugar and cornflour. Add the milk and stir constantly over medium heat until slightly thickened and smooth. Remove from the heat, mix about a third of the hot mixture into the beaten egg yolks. Add the egg yolk mixture to the remaining hot mixture in the saucepan. Cook over low heat for 3 minutes longer. Remove from the heat and add the vanilla and milk chocolate pieces. Stir until the chocolate melts then leave to cool. In a medium-sized bowl, beat the egg whites until stiff but not dry. Fold into the cooled chocolate mixture then spoon into a large bowl. Freeze until almost solid. Beat the cream until stiff. Next, remove the almost frozen chocolate mixture from the freezer and, working quickly so the mixture does not thaw completely, beat until fluffy. Fold in the whipped cream and immediately replace in the freezer. Freeze overnight or until firm. **Makes about 2 litres/3½ pints.**

Butter Mint Ice Cream

Crushed mints and whipping cream add the final exquisite touch.

75 g/3 oz plain chocolate
350 g/12 oz sugar
2 teaspoons cornflour
600 ml/1 pint single cream
300 ml/½ pint milk
generous pinch of salt
4 egg yolks, well beaten
50 g/2 oz finely chopped butter mints
300 ml/½ pint whipping cream

Melt the chocolate and set it aside. In a medium-sized saucepan, combine the sugar and cornflour. Stir in the single cream, milk and salt. Stir constantly over medium heat until the mixture thickens. Remove from heat and stir about one-third of the hot mixture into the beaten egg yolks. Add the egg yolk mixture to the remaining hot mixture in the saucepan. Continue cooking over low heat for 3 minutes. Stir in the melted chocolate then cool. Add the crushed mints and whipping cream. Pour into shallow ice trays or an ice cream machine and freeze. **Makes about 2.25 litres/4 pints.**

Frozen Bananas

50 g/2 oz butter or margarine
175 g/6 oz plain chocolate, broken into pieces
3 tablespoons evaporated milk
6 or 7 bananas
25 g/1 oz finely chopped nuts, if desired

Line a baking tray with waxed paper and set it aside. In an 18 or 20-cm/7 or 8-in pan over low heat and stirring constantly, melt the butter or margarine and chocolate pieces. Stir in the evaporated milk. Remove from the heat. Peel the bananas and insert a skewer into one end of each. Dip the bananas one at a time into the hot chocolate mixture, turning to coat completely. If desired, dip into chopped nuts before the chocolate sets. Place on a prepared baking tray and freeze. If not to be served the same day, freeze the coated bananas in sealed freezer bags or wrap in foil. For a better eating consistency, remove from the freezer 10 minutes before serving. **Serves 6 or 7.**

Frozen Bananas

Mocha Chip Ice Cream

Chocolate flecks appear like magic whey you add hot melted chocolate to the cold cream mixture.

225 g/8 oz sugar
1 tablespoon cornflour
1 tablespoon instant coffee powder
$\frac{1}{8}$ teaspoon salt
1 litre/2 pints single cream
6 eggs, slightly beaten
1 tablespoon vanilla essence
50 g/2 oz plain chocolate

In a medium-sized saucepan, combine the sugar, cornflour, coffee powder and salt. Stir in 600 ml/1 pint of the cream. Stir constantly over low heat until thickened and bubbly. Stir about a third of the hot mixture into the beaten eggs, then add the egg mixture to the remaining hot mixture in the saucepan. Cook and stir 1 minute longer. Chill. Stir in the rest of the cream and the vanilla. Melt the chocolate and while it is hot, pour very slowly into the chilled cream mixture, stirring constantly. Pour into shallow ice trays or an ice cream machine and freeze. **Makes about 2.25 litres/4 pints.**

Ice Cream Italiano

This is so smooth and rich because it's made with a base of Italian-style meringue.

300 ml/$\frac{1}{2}$ pint milk
175 g/6 oz plain chocolate
225 g/8 oz sugar
4 tablespoons water
3 egg whites
$\frac{1}{4}$ teaspoon cream of tartar
300 ml/$\frac{1}{2}$ pint whipping cream

In a small saucepan, heat the milk and chocolate, stirring until the chocolate melts. Simmer for several minutes until the mixture is the consistency of double cream. Set the pan in ice and stir until cool; set aside. In another small saucepan, bring the sugar and water to a boil and continue boiling without stirring until the syrup reaches the soft-ball stage or 115 C, 238 F on a sugar thermometer. While the sugar and water are boiling, beat the egg whites in a large bowl until foamy. Add the cream of tartar and continue beating until stiff peaks form. Gradually pour the syrup, which has reached soft-ball stage, into the egg whites. Continue beating for about 5 minutes or until cool. Fold in the chocolate mixture. Whip the cream and fold into the chocolate mixture. Spoon into a plastic container, a bowl or ice trays, cover and freeze until firm. **Makes about 2.25 litres/4 pints.**

Alaska Pie

175 g/6 oz biscuit crumbs
(13 to 15 biscuits)
50 g/2 oz butter or margarine, melted
1 litre/2 pints mint or coffee ice cream, slightly softened
3 egg whites
$\frac{1}{2}$ quantity Marshmallow Frosting (page 36)
Royal Chocolate Sauce (page 37)

In a small bowl, combine the biscuit crumbs and melted butter or margarine. Press on the bottom and sides of a 23-cm/9-in flan tin. Refrigerate until firm. Spoon ice cream over the chocolate crust. Freeze. Preheat the oven to 230 C/450 F. In a small bowl, beat the egg whites until stiff peaks form. Beat in the Marshmallow Frosting one-quarter at a time. Spoon onto the frozen pie. Spread carefully, sealing to the edge of the crust. Bake for 2 to 3 minutes or until golden. Serve immediately or return to the freezer for several hours or overnight. Serve with chocolate sauce. **Serves 6 to 8.**

Ice Cream Meringue Pie

2 egg whites
100 g/4 oz sugar
$\frac{1}{2}$ teaspoon baking powder
$\frac{1}{4}$ teaspoon salt
50 g/2 oz digestive biscuit crumbs
75 g/3 oz plain chocolate drops
1 litre/2 pints walnut ice cream
150 ml/$\frac{1}{4}$ pint Royal Chocolate Sauce (page 37)
or Hot Fudge Sauce (page 37)

Grease and flour a 23-cm/9-in flan tin; set aside. Set the oven at 180 C, 350 F, gas 4. In a small bowl, beat the egg whites until frothy. Gradually add the sugar and beat until stiff and glossy. Fold in the baking powder, salt, crumbs and chocolate drops. Spoon into the prepared tin, gently building up the side with the back of a spoon. Bake for 20 to 25 minutes. Cool, then fill with ice cream. Spoon chocolate syrup or fudge sauce over. Cut into wedges and serve immediately. **Serves 6 to 8.**

Frozen Mint Cups

100 g/4 oz plain chocolate
225 g/8 oz butter, softened
225 g/8 oz icing sugar
4 eggs
$\frac{1}{2}$ teaspoon peppermint essence

Line 8 cream caramel moulds or custard cups with paper baking cases; set aside. Melt the chocolate and set aside also. In a large bowl, cream the butter and icing sugar until light and fluffy. Add the eggs one at a time, beating after each addition. Stir in the melted chocolate and peppermint essence. Pour into the lined moulds or cups and freeze for several hours. Just before serving turn out onto serving plates. **Serves 8.**

Dark Chocolate Cups

Delectable chocolate cups filled with your favourite ice cream or pudding.

100 g/4 oz plain chocolate
16 to 20 fluted paper baking cases
desired filling

Melt the chocolate in the top of a double boiler over hot but not boiling water. Remove the double boiler from heat but leave the top part over hot water. Use a double thickness of paper cases. Dip a new, clean, dry 1-cm/$\frac{1}{2}$-in brush in melted chocolate. Brush over the bottom and sides of the cases 2–3 mm/$\frac{1}{16}$–$\frac{1}{8}$ in thick, pushing the chocolate into the ridges and smoothing it as much as possible. Place in bun tins or small cups and chill until set. Carefully peel off the paper and fill with the desired filling. **Serves 8 to 10.**

Variation

Light Chocolate Cups: Substitute 75 g/3 oz milk chocolate, broken into pieces and 75 g/3 oz plain chocolate for the 100 g/4 oz plain chocolate. Use 20 to 24 baking cases. **Serves 10 to 12.**

Drinks

There are almost as many products for making chocolate drinks as there are ways to do it. For a quick glass of chocolate milk or a cup of hot cocoa in the morning before school or work, it's handy to have one of the instant chocolate mixes on hand. Some of these are available in individual packets where the mix is pre-measured. Others are sold in larger packets and you measure out the amount needed. Suggested amounts are given in the directions on the packet.

We have included recipes for making traditional hot cocoa or hot chocolate. Try them to see which you like best. For a special-occasion breakfast, French chocolate is a memorable treat.

Chocolate is an ideal partner for many liqueurs when you are creating interesting, unusual after-dinner drinks. They can even take the place of desserts. Your guests will be impressed with your originality and you'll be pleased with the elegant effect achieved with so little work.

Café Bahia (overleaf)

Hot Cocoa

The blend of cocoa and milk produces a very appealing beverage.

3 tablespoons unsweetened cocoa powder
50 g/2 oz sugar
475 ml/16 fl oz milk

In a small saucepan, combine the cocoa and sugar. Pour in a little of the milk, stirring to form a smooth paste. Gradually stir in the remaining milk. Heat over low heat but do not boil. Remove from the heat and beat until foamy. Pour into 3 cups. **Serves 3.**

Hot Chocolate

25 g/1 oz plain chocolate
2 tablespoons water
50 g/2 oz sugar
475 ml/16 fl oz milk
$\frac{1}{4}$ teaspoon vanilla essence

In a small saucepan, combine the chocolate and water. Stir over very low heat until chocolate melts. Add the sugar and stir until blended. Gradually stir in the milk. Heat thoroughly, stirring occasionally. **Serves 3 to 4.**

Café au Lait

450 ml/$\frac{3}{4}$ pint strong coffee
475 ml/16 fl oz milk
3 tablespoons chocolate syrup
150 ml/$\frac{1}{4}$ pint whipping cream
2 tablespoons crème de cacao
grated chocolate

In a medium-sized saucepan, heat the coffee, milk and chocolate syrup. Remove from the heat. While the coffee mixture is heating, whip the cream. Fold in the crème de cacao. Pour the hot coffee mixture into 5 coffee cups or heatproof glasses. Top with whipped cream and grated chocolate. **Serves 5.**

French Chocolate

A superbly elegant treat for eight or second helpings for four.

50 g/2 oz plain chocolate
75 g/3 oz golden syrup
3 tablespoons water
$\frac{1}{2}$ teaspoon vanilla essence
300 ml/$\frac{1}{2}$ pint whipping cream
900 ml/$1\frac{1}{2}$ pints milk

In a small saucepan, stir the chocolate, golden syrup and water over low heat until the chocolate melts and the mixture is smooth. If a few flecks of chocolate remain, beat briefly with a whisk. Stir in the vanilla, then chill. Beat the cream until almost stiff and add the chilled chocolate mixture gradually, continuing to beat until the mixture mounds when dropped from a spoon. Refrigerate. Just before serving, heat the milk until very hot but not boiling. Spoon the whipped cream mixture equally into 8 cups. Fill the cups with hot milk, stir to blend and serve immediately. **Serves 8.**

Café Bahia

A scrumptious after-dinner drink—or a dessert.

450 ml/$\frac{3}{4}$ pint strong coffee
3 tablespoons chocolate syrup
2 tablespoons brandy
2 tablespoons coffee-flavoured liqueur
generous pinch of nutmeg
150 ml/$\frac{1}{4}$ pint whipping cream
2 tablespoons orange liqueur
grated chocolate or grated orange rind

In a small saucepan, heat the coffee, chocolate syrup, brandy, coffee liqueur and nutmeg. While the coffee mixture is heating, whip the cream until stiff. Fold in the orange liqueur. Pour the hot coffee mixture into 4 mugs or heatproof glasses. Top with whipped cream, then grated chocolate or orange rind. **Serves 4.**

Old Amsterdam Coffee

This richly flavoured coffee can be a dessert too.

450 ml/$\frac{3}{4}$ pint strong hot coffee
2 tablespoons white crème de menthe
2 tablespoons mint chocolate liqueur
whipped cream
grated chocolate

Combine the hot coffee with the crème de menthe and mint chocolate liqueur. Pour into 4 small cups or heatproof glasses. Top with whipped cream, then the grated chocolate. Serve immediately. **Serves 4.**

Grasshopper Frappé

600 ml/1 pint chocolate ice cream
3 tablespoons white crème de menthe
3 tablespoons crème de cacao
chocolate curls, if desired

In the blender container, combine the ice cream with the crème de menthe and crème de cacao. Blend until smooth. Pour into 4 small glasses. If desired, sprinkle with the chocolate curls. Serve at once. **Serves 4.**

Banana Eggnog

Terrific as an after-school snack or a quick breakfast.

1 large banana, peeled
1 egg
3 tablespoons sweetened instant cocoa mix
450 ml/$\frac{3}{4}$ pint cold milk

Break the banana into 4 or 5 pieces. In the blender container, combine the banana, egg, cocoa mix and milk. Blend until smooth. **Serves 2.**

Homemade Crème de Cacao

An excellent chocolate liqueur that is both inexpensive and easy to make.

225 g/8 oz sugar
water
25 g/1 oz plain chocolate
$\frac{1}{2}$ teaspoon vanilla essence
300 ml/$\frac{1}{2}$ pint vodka

In a medium-sized saucepan, combine the sugar and water. Boil on a medium-high heat until the mixture is reduced to half its volume, about 20 minutes. About 5 minutes before the syrup is done, melt the chocolate in a 600 ml/1 pint or larger container. Immediately, but very slowly, pour the hot syrup into the melted chocolate, stirring vigorously while pouring. If the mixture is not completely smooth and blended, beat with the mixer or in the blender. Cool the mixture for 30 minutes. Add the vanilla and vodka, blending well. Immediately pour into a bottle or jar with a tight fitting cap or lid. **Makes about 600 ml/1 pint liqueur.**

Black and White Ice Cream Sodas

Purists may use chocolate ice cream instead of vanilla.

150 ml/$\frac{1}{4}$ pint cold milk
3 tablespoons chocolate syrup
4 scoops vanilla ice cream
cold lemon soda or lemonade
whipped cream
2 maraschino cherries

Mix the milk with the chocolate syrup and pour it into 2 tall glasses. Add 1 scoop of ice cream to each glass. Pour in a small amount of cold soda or lemonade; mash the ice cream in each glass with the back of a long-handled spoon. Add a second scoop of ice cream to each glass then fill up the glasses with soda or lemonade. Decorate with whipped cream and a cherry. **Serves 2.**

Index